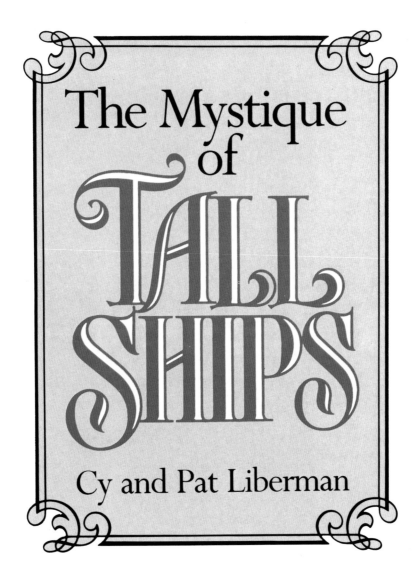

The Mystique of TALL SHIPS

Cy and Pat Liberman

The Middle Atlantic Press

THE MYSTIQUE OF TALL SHIPS

A MIDDLE ATLANTIC PRESS BOOK

Copyright © 1986 by Cy and Pat Liberman

First Middle Atlantic Press printing, November 1986

The Middle Atlantic Press, Inc.
848 Church Street, P.O. Box 945
Wilmington, Delaware 19899
ISBN: 0-912608-28-5

Designed by Emre Kavlakoglu

Printed in Spain by Printer I.G.S.A. Barcelona

Library of Congress Cataloging-in-Publication Data

Liberman, Cy.
    The mystique of tall ships.

    Includes index.
    1. Sailing ships. I. Liberman, Pat. II. Title.
VM145.L47   1986   387.2'23   86-18022
ISBN 0-912608-28-5

Table of Contents

To The Sailing Ship

The slender mast from deck to tip
Holds high the curving clouds of white
That grasp the wind to drive the ship
As gracefully as birds in flight.

She's beautiful in port at ease;
More glorious when she's flushed with motion.
With wind and wave she proudly flees,
Free and happy on the ocean.

Most silently and cleanly done:
The hull divides protesting waves,
And shows it's easy work if one
Is tuned to how the Earth behaves.

The ship: man's knowledge well-refined,
The blend of science, luck and art—
A triumph of the human mind,
A triumph for the human heart.

Dedication

This book is dedicated to lovers of the sea—those who are mesmerized by its sounds and motion, those who love to sail, and especially those who love to see and know about the Tall Ships, some of the most beautiful and graceful of all human creations.

Acknowledgements

We are grateful to many generous people for valuable assistance in producing this book. Stanley Budner originated the idea. Experts in maritime history, building replicas, and sail training, as well as Tall Ships buffs with remarkable libraries, shared information with us. These include Peter Stanford of the National Maritime Historical Society, Norman Brouwer of South Street Seaport Museum, Melbourne Smith of the International Historical Watercraft Society, Captain George Crowninshield of the American Sail Training Association, Bernie Klay of Sea Heritage Foundation, Donald W. Callender, Jr., John Dossett, Captain Charles M. Quinlan, and Malcolm MacKenzie. We thank Thomas E. Miller and Pamela Hoffman for translation, Shari Gallagher-Phalan for typing, and Joan Ware Colgan for research, Richard S. Brooks for editing and encouragement, Nicolas Liberman, and E.I. duPont de Nemours & Co., Inc., Edge Moor Plant, for photographs.

In any compilation of facts and figures of this magnitude, there is a high probability of imperfection. Any errors that turn up are strictly our own responsibility and we trust will be reported for correction later.

C. & P. L.

Preface

Everyone enjoys the beauty and majesty of Tall Ships. The evidence is the swarming masses of people who crowd the waterfronts and pepper the waterways with boats whenever there is an opportunity to see the Tall Ships. The purpose of this book is to add to that enjoyment by supplying ship-watchers with pertinent background to enlarge the picture they are seeing. Here they will find facts on individual ships and the roles they play today, as well as the history of Tall Ships and their part in the development of the civilized world. In addition, there are details on the design and rigging of different types of sailing vessels of the past and present.

The ship-watcher, after reading this book, will not only be able to identify the ships as they sail past, but he or she will enjoy them again and again in memory with the help of the illustrations.

The grand dames of the Tall Ships are the school ships—the largest sailing vessels in active use today. They are gorgeous reminders of the fleets of sailing vessels that transported humans and their cargo on all the oceans of the world before the advent of steamships and aircraft. Those great ships are few in number now, but with their ballooning clouds of square-rigged sails, they are perhaps the most fascinating of all sailing craft to observe.

There is also tremendous interest in the larger schooners and other yachts—all billowing beauties on the water as they gather the breeze and bend it to their purposes in one of the most challenging and invigorating of human endeavors, the art of sailing.

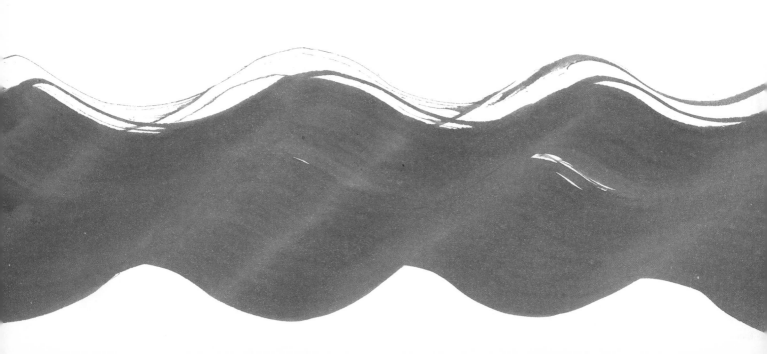

The
Mystique
of
Tall
Ships

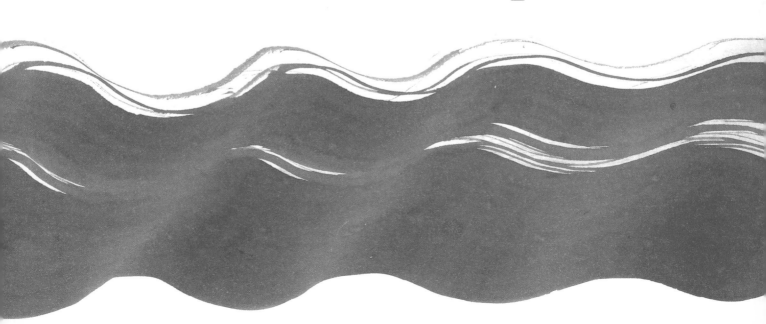

The ability of humans of ancient times to create, without our advanced technology, objects of beauty and utility is a source of wonder to thoughtful people today. We view with amazement the feat of the Egyptians in building the pyramids thousands of years ago without a crane to lift those mammoth blocks of rock. Ancient Greeks shaped stones into handsome buildings and splendid sculpture. Through the ages and throughout the world, a vast array of human creations have combined art and technical skill in ways that modern people look upon with awe. Not the least of these inspired creations are ships.

On our own continent, most Americans have a deep admiration and a kind of patriotic pride in the record of the early settlers from Europe who used the axe so skillfully to cut their way through the wilderness, then used the adze so masterfully to transform those trees into ships. We marvel at their resourcefulness and craftmanship. These are important elements in the mystique of Tall Ships.

Beyond the beauty of clouds of set sails, beyond the bewildering maze of rigging, another element in the enchantment of the Tall Ships is a linkage we feel with our past. Wherever our immigrant ancestors came from, many came by sail, and we feel a reverence for our roots as symbolized by the square-rigged ships we see at seaport museums or coastal celebrations.

That many of our forbears came here, some in chains, most in miserably overloaded, insubstantial ships, awash with disease and constant discomfort, contributes to the mystique, and history comes alive. One can look up at the mighty yards, the highflung sails and picture "the flung spray, the blown spume, the seagulls flying" and hear "the wind's song and the white sail's shaking" of Masefield's evocative poem. Whatever reason our ancestors had for coming across to these shores, that romance and adventure is expressed today in our affection for Tall Ships.

Add to this our love of the sea—conscious and subconcious. Some of us are all but hypnotized by looking at the sea, watching the endless motion of the waves and swells. Others are drawn to go upon the sea in boats and ships of all kinds—anything that will float and let an individual feel surrounded by and close to the water, out on a small part of an immense pathway that connects all corners of the earth. We know the Tall Ships could go anywhere on that broad pathway, driven by the wind alone in some half understood and half mysterious way.

To many who love the sea and also love small boats, the sheer size and strange rigging on the old sailing ships are matters of wonder. A 72-foot ketch seems impressively large. But a schooner twice as long and a bark three or four times as long are matters for amazement. We love sailing boats. We are in awe of sailing ships.

We are no less affected by the materials used in the construction of these vessels. At home with modern fiberglass, aluminum and wood of a modest thickness, citizens of the 20th Century are often overwhelmed by the weight of the iron, steel and timbers in the frames and planks of old ships. Can a hull that heavy really sail? Obviously, they not only sailed—they circumnavigated our earth!

And then we look at the rigs. How could those oldtime skippers get where they wanted to go with square sails? Clearly, they mastered the prevailing winds and currents, applied the sailing lore of generations, and forced those rigs to carry them to their far away destinations and back. The more we know about boats of our own time, the more we marvel at the ships of an earlier era and the men who sailed them.

All those strands and perhaps many more are woven into the fabric of emotion that constitutes the mystique of the Tall Ships.

How
Tall
Is
Tall?

How to Identify Tall Ships

What do people mean when they speak of the Tall Ships?

They usually mean the square-riggers and other large sailing vessels—all those watercraft that are like swans among a flock of ducks. This book is about both—the square-rigged ships that are the stars of all gatherings of Tall Ships and the big schooners and other larger-than-ordinary yachts that are featured players at those gatherings.

These ships are fairly rare. People rush to see them when the opportunities arise, all too infrequently.

Not only are viewers thrilled at the sight of the Tall Ships, but they find it a pleasant sport to identify them by rig and look up their dimensions. The material in the following pages provides easy-to-understand guidelines and dimensions.

This book does not place the Tall Ships in classes, nor does it rate them. They all deserve Class 1-A, four stars and gold medals.

One dimension given needs some explanation—the length overall of many vessels. It may be interpreted several ways. The legal definition of "overall length" excludes bowsprits and other attachments to the hull. Most Tall Ships do have bowsprits, however, and it is pertinent to know how long the ships are, including all projections. Technically that figure is known as "sparred length." Owners frequently report it as overall length.

The term "sparred length" is sometimes used in this book, but other terms such as "length overall" or simply "length" are also used. Unless "length on deck" is specified, the only length figure used here is sparred length. Put simply, if you were putting a Tall Ship alongside a pier, that is how much space it would require.

Once again, a Tall Ship is any large sailing vessel, square-rigged or not, and any square-rigged vessel regardless of size.

And finally, how large is large? How tall is tall? One need not draw an arbitrary line. Instead, the descriptions in these pages include the more interesting and unusual ships that shipwatchers sometimes have opportunities to see.

The smaller yachts that can be seen by the hundreds in any popular harbor are not listed.

Brigantine

Barkentine

Brig

Bark

The Types of Ships

Part of the fun of seeing Tall Ships is in being able to identify them. It is the same thing with stars, birds and flowers. One enjoys being able to say, "There's Orion's belt," or, "Look at that male goldfinch," or "Here's a bloodroot."

To identify ships, the first step is to know the rig. Many of the larger, sail-training vessels in use today are *barks* (also spelled *barques*), *full-rigged ships* or *barkentines* and *brigantines*. *The difference are in the number of masts they have and kinds of sails on those masts.

Does the ship have at least one mast that has nothing on it but square sails? If the answer is yes, the next step is to count the number of masts. If the vessel has three or more masts, she must be a *bark,* a full-rigged ship or a barkentine. If she has only two masts, she must be a brigantine or a *brig.*

The next step in any identification process is to see where the square sails are, and, after we understand the difference, where any fore-and-aft sails are. Square sails are sometimes fairly square but are more often rectangular. They are held aloft on *yards,* which are horizontal *spars* attached to the mast. Square sails and their yards in normal position are aligned with the width of the ship, whereas fore-and-aft sails, as the term implies, are aligned with the ship's length.

*Nautical terms italicized when first used are defined in the Glossary.

Gaff Rigged Sloop

Schooner

Topsail Schooner

Fullrigged Ship

Marconi Sloop

Cutter

Ketch

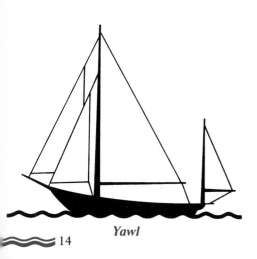

Yawl

Lateen Rig

They are the kind of sails we see on modern sailboats, small and large—sails which, when relaxed, follow the centerline of the boat from bow to stern. These include large sails attached to the aft side of the mast and to a *boom*—a *spar* at the bottom of the sail. Suppose you are standing at the waterfront watching a parade of Tall Ships, and one comes along. You count the masts; she has three. You look at the rigging-aha! There are square sails on all three masts—that vessel is a full-rigged ship. Perhaps she is *Amerigo Vespucci, Christian Radich,* or *Libertad.* You can tell by the national flag or ensign, or you may be able to read the name with the help of binoculars.

As the ship goes by, check to see if she has a small fore-and-aft sail on her last mast, called the *mizzen.* She may have, but if she also has square sails on that mast, she is still considered a full-rigged ship. However if she has no square sails on the mizzen, and has fore-and-aft sails there, she is a *bark* like *Eagle, Mircea* or *Sagres II.* Along comes another three-masted vessel. This one has square sails on the first mast only; without a doubt she is a barkentine such as *Palinuro,* or *Gazela of Philadelphia.* A very large ship with four masts, square-rigged on only the first, would probably be *Esmeralda,* the largest sail-training ship in the Western Hemisphere and a rare example of a four masted barkentine.

Remember that any three-masted vessel with square sails occupying all of one or more of her masts must be a full-rigged ship, a bark or a barkentine.

Among two masted vessels with square sails, the question is how to distinguish between a brig and a brigantine. If the ship is square-rigged on both her masts, she is a brig—a rather rare rig. The Indian Navy has a brig, *Varuna.*

If, on the other hand, the ship is square-rigged on the foremast only and has a fore-and-aft sail on her mainmast, she is a brigantine, like the new *Spirit of Chemainus.* A brigantine may or may not have a square sail above the fore-and-aft sail on her mainmast, which is the higher of the two masts.

Sometimes the term *hermaphrodite brig* is used: it means brigantine. The term was used long ago with the excuse that the rig is half that of a brig and half that of a *schooner.*

The fore-and-aft sail on the rigs just described is held up by a *gaff*—a slanting spar at the top of the sails. Such a sail is *gaff-rigged.* It has four sides in contrast to the more modern three-sided sails commonly used today. Gaff-rigged sails resemble a triangle with the top corner cut off diagonally. However, when you look at a traditional gaff-rigged sail with a smaller topsail over it, the two together look like a triangular sail in two parts, separated by the slanting gaff.

The same is true of the fore-and-aft sail at the stern of the bark or sometimes, of a full-rigged ship. That sail is called a *spanker,* and may be in two or three sections forming a triangle separated by one or two gaffs. The topmost section is called the *topsail* or *gaff topsail.* If a spanker is in two parts aside from the topsail, they are called the *upper and lower spanker.*

Does the Tall Ship you are watching have at least one mast that has nothing but square sails on it? If the answer is no, the ship is a fore-and-aft rigged vessel which may be one of at least seven types: *schooner, ketch, yawl, sloop, cutter, cat* or *lateen-rigged.*

The next step in this identification sport is to count the masts. If there are four and the ship is large, the vessel is a *schooner* and is probably *Juan Sebastian de Elcano,* one of the few large, four-masted schooners in existence. If there are three masts, the vessel is also a schooner. If there are two, she may be a schooner, a ketch, a yawl· or a cat-ketch.

Schooner Rig

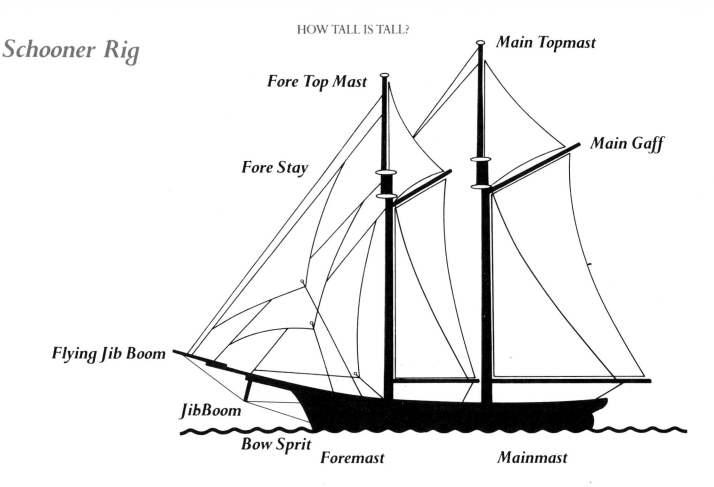

Main Topmast

Fore Top Mast

Main Gaff

Fore Stay

Flying Jib Boom

JibBoom

Bow Sprit
Foremast
Mainmast

Next question: Which of the two masts is higher? If the second one is higher, the vessel is a schooner. The shorter one is called the *foremast* and the other is the *mainmast*.

Many schooners have extra sails at the top of the mast and are dubbed *topsail schooners*. Those that have no topsail are sometimes called *bald*. At times, the topsails are square sails, as in the *Californian* and *Pride of Baltimore*. This does not make the ship a square-rigged vessel.

In addition to sails on their mainmast, most rigs described in this book have sails before the mainmast, called *staysails* or *jibs*. These are triangular sails set on a stay (usually a wire) between two masts or between a mast and the deck or the bowsprit.

When the stay runs from the foremast to the bowsprit, the staysail is similar to a jib and may be one of a series of sails supplementing one or more jibs.

Suppose the two-masted vessel has its higher mast forward. Then she is a *ketch* or *yawl* rather than a schooner. Each has a tall mainmast and a shorter mizzen or jiggermast further aft. On a yawl, the mizzenmast and its sail are smaller than on a ketch of similar size, but the technical difference is in the placement of the mast. In the yawl, the mast is aft of the rudderpost; in the ketch, it is forward of that post.

There is one more two-masted vessel that is easily recognized—the *cat-ketch*. In this rig, both masts are usually the same size. The foremast is far forward in the ship's bow and carries the mainsail. In many cat-ketches, the masts are unstayed (no fastening lines to the deck).

Schooner Sails

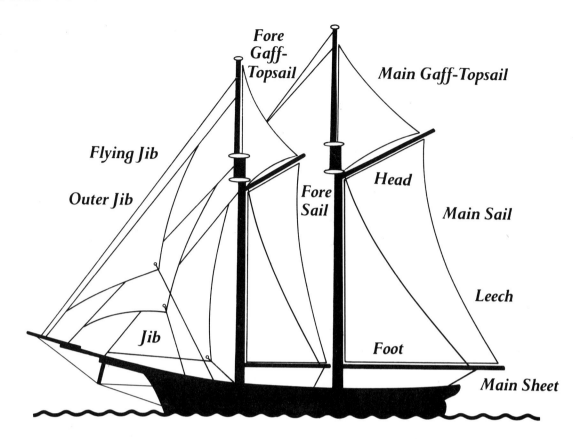

A ship with only one mast must be a *sloop,* a *cutter,* a *catboat,* or a *lateen rigged* vessel. The sloop, in addition to the mainsail, normally has one working sail—a jib—forward of the mast, whereas the cutter has two—a jib and a staysail. Also, the cutter's mast is usually closer to the center of the boat. The sloop is the most popular rig on recreational sail boats today. Many sailors contend that the sloop rig is the most efficient for sailing upwind, and a high proportion of racing boats are sloop-rigged. The cat rig employs a single mast far forward in the ship, and a single sail, often gaff-rigged.

The lateen rig uses a triangular sail suspended from a long yard, set obliquely to the mast. Many Mediterranean and Nile River craft, and many from other parts of the world, past and present, are lateen-rigged. In the United States, it is seen on the popular Sunfish and other small recreational boats.

Square Sails

Each sail on a square-rigged ship, or any other sailing vessel, has a name. When the skipper orders crew members to furl the *main skysail,* there can be no doubt which sail he wants rolled up and secured. On a full-rigged ship or a bark, there are likely to be from 30 to 34 different sails, each with a name indicating which mast it is on as well as its position on that mast.

If the ship has six levels of square sails on the mainmast, the lowest and largest sail is called the *mainsail* (pronounced mayn'sl) or *main course.* Above the mainsail is the *main lower topsail* (pronounced tops'l), and over that flies the *main upper topsail.* At the fourth level up from the deck is the *main topgallant,* followed by the *main royal.* All the way at the top is the *top skysail* (pronounced skys'l).

Today's curious dockside observer may have a casual interest in knowing something about the sails and the running rigging of a square-rigged ship, but a brief brush with the marine vocabulary may be enough. Each sail and each yard has its own set of lines coming down to the deck in what is, to the uninitiated, an extremely complex array, like a gigantic spider web. Each line has its purpose in sailing the vessel and is fastened around its own *belaying pin.*

However, for the seaman working on a square-rigged ship in the old days, it was absolutely essential to "learn the ropes"—and quickly! Every crew member had to know all the lines and to be able to locate the right belaying pin for each line—in double quick time! To make sure seamen learned, it was customary for officers to devise complex drills that chased the seamen from bow to stern, locating pins as orders were shouted. Punishment, some outrageously cruel, was the lot of crew members who could not match line to belaying pin. The most inhuman punishment was the famous keel-haul, which meant tying the slow learner, throwing him overboard, dragging him under the vessel and up the other side.

The glossary of this book contains definitions of many of the terms used in identifying the sails and rigging, and supplements the illustrations. Informative displays on the rigging of square-rigged ships, showing the complexities of both the running rigging and standing rigging, which supports the masts, may be studied at the maritime museums.

Tonnage

One measure used in describing the size of a ship is the figure stating its tonnage, but there are several kinds of tonnage. Figures for gross and net tonnage report on the cubic volume of cargo the ship can carry. These figures give the ship's capacity, not its weight. The displacement tonnage gives the ship's weight—how much water it displaces in floating. Where the information is available, we give the displacement rather than the capacity, to indicate the size of ships.

The History of Sail

When one considers that about three-fourths of the earth's surface is covered by water, it comes as no surprise that earthlings learned to move about in boats at a very early stage. It can even be argued that humans learned to sail before they learned to farm. In any event, people have been using the wind to push their boats for thousands of years.

Hints on the earliest watercraft come from models, pictures and artifacts found by archeologists on land and under water. A clay model found in Mesopotamia–the ancient land between the Tigris and Euphrates Rivers which is currently Iraq–depicted the earliest known sailing vessel from about 3,500 B.C. Three hundred years later, a vase made in Egypt depicted a papyrus raft with a square sail.

The earliest actual boat discovered is one built of cedarwood around 2,650 B.C., found in an airtight and watertight tomb in Egypt. It is shaped like the papyrus raft–·long and slender, with a bottom curving up in crescent shape at stem and stern. This oldest known boat probably never floated, for it is believed to be a burial craft, intended for voyages after death by the Pharoah Cheops. But it gives solid evidence of the size and shape of early Egyptian vessels. It is about 142 feet long.

Paintings and models of other ancient Egyptian watercraft show oblong sails placed far forward, indicating they were used only for running before the wind. In Egypt, the prevailing wind is from the north, making it likely these vessels sailed up the Nile against the current and returned with oars supplementing the current. Egyptian wooden hulls were made with planks fastened to each other by tenons shaped like hourglasses, similar to the "butterfly keys" used by today's woodworkers, as well as by the use of pegs and rope lashing. Most of the ships were flat-bottomed. There were no ribs in the early vessels to support the hull planks; later, ribs were inserted, after the shell-like hulls were built.

As early as 2,000 B.C. sailing vessels were built in Crete. It is believed that those ships built in Phoenicia (in Asia Minor) and in ancient Greece and Rome all had hulls built as shells with the planks fastened together and ribs inserted in the last stage of hull construction. The system of building a ship's skeleton by fastening ribs to a keel before attaching planks came centuries later.

In the 6th and 5th Centuries B.C., ancient Greece had both merchant ships and warships and some that combined both functions. Greek ships of that time were built of pine, with yards of spruce. Rectangular sails were of linen, while the ropes used to support the mast and control the sails were of flax or hemp. Unlike the earlier Egyptian boats, they had long, straight keels. There were usually two oars at the stern, one on each side, for steering. The use of dead-eyes and lanyards to tighten the standing rigging apparently started with vessels of ancient Rome, most of them with two masts.

An ancient jar, or amphora, found in the northern Aegean Sea is decorated with a clear carving of a lateen sail–a type that has remained popular to the present in the Mediterranean. Other evidence from the northern Aegean shows ships rigged with spritsails. This is a fore-and-aft sail on a mast stretched by a diagonal spar called a sprit. These are the two earliest known indications of the use of fore-and-aft sails in a world of ships dominated for centuries by square sails.

Some Roman ships had a short mast forward, slanting at about 45 degrees. At the forward end, a small square sail on a yard was hung forward of the bow, where it was probably helpful in steering. The use of foresails of this type persisted into the 17th Century.

Remains of ancient Roman ships examined through the work of underwater archeologists show the hull plans fastened together with mortise and tenon joints, as the earlier Egyptian and Greek ships were built, and that frames were added after the shell was constructed. Treenails (pegs) and copper nails were used to fasten planks to frames.

The Dark Ages are indeed dark regarding the history of sailing ships in the Mediterranean for about 600 years after the Romans until evidence comes to light on vessels of the 9th century A.D. The typical vessel was rigged with a triangular lateen sail on a yard longer than the vessel itself, suspended from a short mast raking slightly forward, supported by shrouds. This is a *felucca,* which is still sailed today. On the 9th century ship, steering was still done by means of two oars, one on each side, as in the ancient vessels.

While shipbuilding was progressing in the Mediterranean area, an independent learning experience was going on in northern Europe. The fundamental difference was in the method of fastening planks to build hulls. Whereas in the Mediterranean locale the planks were joined edge to edge, the Nordic builders overlapped the planks. In modern terms, the Nordic vessels were clinker-built, while the others were carvel built.

One of the characteristics of the early Nordic vessels was the use of a cutwater—a plank extending the stem and keel forward. The same feature appeared on some early Mediterranean boats. The Nordic merchant ship of the 7th Century was an open boat with a square sail mounted amidships on a single yard, and with room for seven or eight oarsmen. The rudder was a long oar mounted on the stern. It is believed this "steer-board" is the derivation of the term *starboard.* The ships were double-enders, with an extension at the stern similar to the cut-water at the bow.

Much is known about the appearance of Viking ships because of the astonishing fact that well-preserved ships of the 9th and 10th Centuries have been retrieved from the waters of the outer Oslo Fyord area. These are the famous *Oseberg, Gokstad* and *Tune* ships, which were buried with rulers of the period. The *Oseberg* ship was built about 800 A.D.; the others about 850 to 900 A.D. The *Oseberg* ship is the first Scandinavian vessel known to have a sail; it could also be rowed with 15 pairs of oars. The ship is 70 feet long and 16.7 feet broad. Built of oak, it has 12 planks on either side of the keel. The keel connects with a carved stem which curves back inboard and ends with a carved scroll. The ship has ribs which were added after the clinker-built shell was assembled. This appears to have been a pleasure craft.

When one speaks of carving on wood in the Viking ships and the sophisticated joints in the wood of ancient Egyptian vessels, it is well to recall the basic materials available to humans for use as tools. In the broadest scale, the Stone Age existed 10,000 years ago; the Bronze Age started about 5,000 years ago, and humans reached the Iron Age about 3,000 years ago. Iron rivets were used on the Oseberg ship.

The *Gokstad* ship is larger than the *Oseberg* ship, with 16 planks on each side. It is about 80 feet long and was rowed by 32 men. Its large square sail could be turned into a fore-and-aft position so that the vessel could tack, and a spar was used in the manner of the modern whisker pole to push forward on the leading edge of the sail. The seaworthiness of the *Gokstad* ship was demonstrated in 1893, when a replica sailed across the Atlantic in 28 days. Viking warships were larger than these burial vessels and had as many as 80 oarsmen.

An important development in ship design occurred in the 12th Century, when the steering oar gave way to the outboard rudder, hung on the stern. The earliest indication of such a change appears in a relief at Winchester Cathedral in England, showing a boat being steered with a rudder and tiller.

Ships of the 13th and 14th Centuries in England and northern Europe, including Germany, began to have platforms fore and aft, apparently for stationing crew members to fight off pirates or enemies. A drawing of a ship from Danzig in Germany, from about 1400, shows several new features. First, the forecastle is triangular instead of square. Second, at the upper end of the mast is a "top," a basket-like structure that could be used by a lookout. Third, ratlines appeared on the shrouds, providing a means of climbing to the top. The ideas of using square sails, castles fore-and-aft and stern rudders reached the Mediterranean in the 14th Century.

The next development in the Mediterranean was the use of a small triangular sail near the stern to aid in steering. Soon, ships from that region had three masts—in addition to the mainmast, carrying a square sail, there was a small square sail on the bowsprit and a slightly larger triangular sail on the mizzenmast. Such a ship, from Portugal, is pictured on a bowl from the early 15th Century; it also has the basket-like top on the mainmast, with a ladder aft of the mast, instead of ratlines.

Further development in size and complexity led to the *caravels* and *carracks* of the 15th and 16th Centuries. Details on these ships are scarce. Some had three masts, others four, and they used a combination of square and lateen sails. The caravel was a very beamy ship; the beam was about one-half the length of the keel.

While the term caravel has been applied to small earlier ships, it is used here to identify those round-hulled vessels with a square stern and a rounded bow that were the first sailing vessels used by western Europeans to face the open ocean on voyages of exploration. Columbus used caravels in his small fleet and also a carrack—a predecessor of the caravel. Magellan used a fleet of carracks.

Columbus' *Santa Maria* was a three-masted carrack about 78 feet long with a beam of 26 feet. The ship is believed to have displaced about 51 tons. She was a round ship, very high at both bow and stern. There was a square sail hanging from the bowsprit, a square sail on the foremast, two square sails on the mainmast and a lateen sail on the mizzenmast. *Santa Maria* was armed with 15th Century cannons and crossbows.

Information from Columbus's log indicates that his ship *Nina* was a caravel about 71 feet long with a beam of 21 feet, displacing about 53 tons. Unlike *Santa Maria*, the *Nina* at first had three lateen sails. The triangular sails were later replaced by square sails. Columbus sailed aboard *Nina* on his second trip.

A third vessel in the fleet, *Pinta,* was a caravel with two square sails on the first two masts and a lateen sail on the third. She was about 65 feet long, about 20 feet in the beam and displaced about 50 tons. The two caravels carried no cannon.

Until the introduction of gunpowder, the same ships could be used for battle, trade and military transport. But putting guns on ships in the 14th Century changed the nature of warfare. Soon heavily armed warships were differentiated from merchant ships. Because of the weight of the cannons, the ships had to be bigger and heavier. During the 15th Century, warships generally increased from about 250 tons displacement in the early years to about 1,000 tons at the close of the century.

Early in the 16th Century, the idea of cutting gunports in the sides of ships was adopted, along with watertight lids to close the low ports in rough weather. That brought the weight of guns lower in the ship and improved stability.

Merchant ships also grew during this period as the ability to build larger ships advanced. There was demand for larger ships to carry merchandise from China, India, Persia and other eastern countries whose goods came over land by camel caravan routes to Mediterranean ports. Meanwhile, in the 15th Century, important strides were made in knowledge about navigation, including the first construction of a globe, mapping the known world and suggesting that all the unknown parts could be reached by the oceans.

The time was right for daring seamen to venture out upon the seas. Portuguese ships rounded the western bulge of Africa in 1434, and went around the Cape of Good Hope by 1488. In 1498, a Portuguese squadron under the command of Vasco da Gama reached India. Columbus, with his three ships, was trying to reach India by a western route when he discovered the islands later called the West Indies. The vessels used in these great voyages of exploration were relatively small ships—from 30 to 90 tons. It was important that they not be too deep; they drew only about six feet. Columbus liked best his smallest ship, *Nina.*

After Portugal and Spain showed the way, England, France and Holland followed them into exploration. Holland reached the East Indies. Cartier, from France, sailed up the St. Lawrence River looking for a route to China. Instead, he found a rich fur trade with Canada. England discovered Newfoundland in 1497; Balboa reached the Pacific in 1513. No one could find a way to Cathay, as China was called, through the great mass of land that later turned out to be North and South America. Magellan did find a way around it in the world's first circumnavigation. At the same time (1519-22), he demonstrated the vast size of the Pacific Ocean, (although he did not live to finish the great voyage himself).

Within a few decades, these voyages of discovery brought an explosion of knowledge about the world and opened the way for a vast growth in trading. In turn, that produced a need for large ships in the 16th Century, when the caravel was gradually replaced by the larger carrack, the *galleon* and the full-rigged ship.

The galleon was more slender than the carrack, with the beam thinned down to about one-third the length of the keel. On the galleon, the high forecastle was all inboard; on the earlier ships it had extended beyond the bow. Also, the castles on the caravel were high, apparently for boarding enemy warships. The galleons had better guns, less dependence on boarding and lower castles.

Galleons often did have a projection beyond the bow, but it was an extension of the deck called the beak-head, and was separate from the higher forecastle. The galleon had four masts with a combination of square and lateen sails. A Venetian description from 1550 puts the length of a galleon from stem to stern at 135 feet. The British ships that defeated the Spanish Armada in 1588 were galleons. Each had three levels of square sails on the fore and mainmasts and lateen sails on shorter masts at the stern, in addition to a small sail on the bowsprit. The forecastle had one deck, but there were three levels of decks rising at the stern, ending in a small poopdeck. A long pivoting lever called the whipstaff, attached to the tiller, was used for steering.

A model of a late 16th Century Flemish galleon has the foremast forward of the the forecastle. This ship has a cathead at the main deck level for raising and lowering the heavy anchor. The ship is heavily ornamented with carving, gilding and painting. Galleons generally had square sterns while earlier ships had round sterns.

The galleon represented a major development in sailing vessel design. During the rest of the life of square-rigged ships, the changes were mere refinements in hull and rigging, with the use of higher masts with more sails, the addition of the fore-and-aft staysails between the masts, jibs at the long bowsprit, and particularly in the 19th Century clippers, the development of the graceful, narrow hull.

Probably the most illustrious galleon in history was *Golden Hind*, the three-masted vessel that was the first English ship to circumnavigate the world. The voyage, under Sir Francis Drake, started in 1577 and required almost three years. The 100-ton *Golden Hind* was about 90 feet long on deck and had a beam of 14 feet. She carried 26 guns and a crew of 146. The sails included a small squaresail on the bowsprit, two square sails on the foremast and mainmast, and a lateen sail on the mizzen. There were two full length decks in addition to the hold and the castles. The crew's toilet, known as the *head*, was on part of the beakhead. This remained the location of the crew's toilet for many years.

One type of vessel worthy of a quick mention in the history of sail is the *galleass*, a cross between a large sailing vessel with a lateen rig and a galley with a multitude of oarsmen. There have been galleys at many stages of history—in classical times and up to the 17th Century. One from Venice apparently was rowed by 240 men—five at each of 48 oars. The large galley and the galeass both looked a bit like centipedes.

The appearance of 17th Century ships of northern Europe is best illustrated, without doubt, by *Vasa*, the Swedish ship of 1628 that capsized at the start of her first voyage. Raised from the water at Stockholm in 1961, *Vasa* has since been restored and kept in a magnificent dry dock museum. She is a three-masted galleon, 230 feet long, displacing 1,400 tons and carrying 12,375 square feet of sails. Her main and mizzen masts are raked aft, but her foremast is vertical. She carried 66 cannons and mortars, which may have been her undoing—too many heavy guns on her upper deck, resulting in top-heaviness.

During the 17th Century, the British developed the idea of the battle line—a single file—as the combat tactic for warships. Ships in the battle line tried to maintain the same speed and to maneuver in the same way. The British classified their warships by firepower: the first-rate ship had more than 90 guns; the second-rate had 80 or more and the third-rate had 50 or more. Those were the fighting ships. A fourth-rate ship had 38 or more guns and was used for escort work and exploration. The fifth-rate ship with over 18 guns was also used for exploration and for signalling. Then there was a sixth-rate ship, with more than six guns, used mainly for coastal patrol work.

The ship of the line was the dominant warship for about two centuries, but it became obsolete with the development of larger guns. It was phased out during the 1870-80 decade when the age of sail was nearing its end.

European ships of the 17th Century were heavily built, often with double frames. These ships were built mainly of oak; it required about 2,000 oak trees to build one. Spars, however, were made of fir, a soft wood. Tapered wooden dowels were used to fasten the planking to the frames. Warships were often double-planked and might have had up to two feet of oak in their sides to withstand bombardment. A coating of tar was applied below the waterline. British hulls were copper-plated starting in 1761.

During the 17th Century, ships, including warships, were highly decorated with gilded carvings, statues, and elaborate lanterns. By about 1750, the practice of decorating ships ceased, except for figureheads.

The wheel for steering came into use about 1705. Around 1750, the long jibboom became a feature of sailing vessels, and with it came the use of jibs and flying jibs instead of the square sail formerly carried on the short bowsprit. Also in this period, the spanker—a fore-and-aft sail at the stern—began to be widely adopted. This became a feature of all full-rigged ships and the barks that came later.

Some warships in the 17th Century were called *frigates*. The term was applied to different warships; frequently it meant a full-rigged man-of-war with only one full deck of guns.

Holland had a large merchant fleet estimated at 10,000 vessels during the 17th Century. One of the more popular designs was the *fluyt* (sometimes spelled flute), a three-masted, fairly narrow vessel with a round stern and flat bottom. Two masts were square rigged, with two sails on each; the mizzen had a single lateen sail.

The British used a ship called a *pinnace*, which differed from the fluyt by having a flat stern. The pinnace was similar to a full-rigged ship, but smaller. There was considerable variety among ships in use in the 17th Century, and from then on throughout the history of sail.

The brigantine, the two-masted vessel with square sails on both masts, also appeared in the 17th Century. So did the first sailing vessel that would fit the modern definition of schooner—a Dutch vessel that was fore-and-aft rigged in a sea of square sails. The first American schooner is said to have been built at Gloucester, Massachusetts, about 1713.

During the same century, pirates of North Africa used a fore-and-aft rigged vessel, called a *xebec*, (pronounced zeebec) with three lateen sails and a jib. The xebecs had low, slender hulls of shallow draft and were excellent sailers. Similar vessels appeared in other countries, including Spain, which used them to fight the pirates.

European navies of the 18th Century built warships they called frigates, and the new American nation did the same. The U.S. Frigates *Constellation* and *Constitution* are examples still in existence. Some smaller warships of the same period, rigged like frigates with three masts, were called sloops. The term has nothing to do with the modern use of "sloop."

Wreck of the H.M. Frigate Guerriere

Photo by Mark Sexton, Peabody Museum of Salem

For every victor in sea warfare there was a loser. When Constitution *earned the name "Old Ironsides," the greater damage was sustained by H.M. Frigate* Guerriere, *here immortalized in a painting by William James Aylward.*

In other developments of that century, the square stern was generally succeeded by the rounded stern, and the fore and stern castles were gradually lowered. In some vessels toward the end of the century, the beak-head was removed in favor of a straight stem.

The customary decoration of the bow of a ship with a carved and often gilded figurehead originated with French ships in the 16th Century, and the practice persisted until steamships took over the seas late in the 19th Century. There is a huge collection of figureheads in the Mariners' Museum at Newport News, Virginia.

Photo by Mark Sexton, Peabody Museum of Salem

Sailing vessels built in the Colonial period of the United States were similar to those in England at the same time, but usually of smaller size. A popular type was the sloop, which combined fore-and-aft sails and square sails. These early American sloops had a single mast, carrying a gaff-rigged mainsail in addition to a square mainsail or course, a square topsail and two or three jibs on a long jibboom. There were many ships called brigantines, but how they were rigged is not clear, and many ships would fall into the current definition of topsail schooner. There were also early ketches in the 17th Century, with a combination of square and fore-and-aft sails.

The American concern for speed was applied to sailing vessels from early Colonial days. The point then was to have small but fast ships which could successfully evade the British and smuggle goods to the American settlements. Many of the ships were schooners, and the same type of vessel was used later, when the new nation was glad to rely on privateers in time of war.

Privateers were privately-owned vessels given a commission or "letter of marque" by the government to capture enemy merchant ships and keep the ships and cargo as prizes—in other words, legalized piracy. They were usually lightly armed and speedy, carrying relatively large crews to board and take over captured vessels. They ran a lucrative but dangerous business, especially during the War of 1812.

Some of the so-called Baltimore clippers were used as privateers. The term *clipper* means a fast ship, and has nothing to do with the rig. The *Pride of Baltimore* was a replica of this type of ship—a topsail schooner relying entirely on fore-and-aft sails, except for a square topsail. Some of the same fast schooners were used in the slave trade.

Many different schooners have flown the U.S. ensign, varying mostly in hull design, less frequently in the rig. For the most part, the earlier ships had blunt, rounded bows, and the later ones have sharper, finer lines at the bow. Some authorities list as many as 11 types of American and Canadian schooners; the differences are mainly the lines of the hulls. Among the names used to describe these schooners are the "Chebaccao," "Pinky," "Fredonia" and "Nova Scotia" types.

The race for speed in ships larger than schooners brought about the design and construction of the clipper ships, which evolved in mid-19th Century America. An early example of a clipper—although there is no "first clipper"—was *Rainbow*, designed by John W. Griffiths and launched in 1845. This ship and others like her demonstrated that speed, formerly considered an attribute of smaller vessels such as schooners, could be achieved in larger merchant ships. Shipbuilders accomplished it by piling more sails on raked, higher masts and wider yards, and still more canvass, when the wind was right, by the use of studding sails. They also modified the hulls, making them longer and more slender throughout, and concave at the bow—all designed to support safely their towering rigs.

The early clippers could carry 750 tons of cargo; later ones had two or three times that capacity, and some were more than 200 feet long. With their lithe lines and clouds of white sails, clippers were beautiful creations that also filled a pressing need for swifter transportation by water. This was far from an overnight achievement, but a gradual evolution, as are most ship designs.

The discovery of gold in California in 1848 created the urgent demand for ships to get both would-be gold miners and supplies of food and other materials to the West Coast. Sailing, even sailing around treacherous Cape Horn, was preferred to the hardships of the alternatives—the long, dangerous journey by wagon train from the East Coast, or the trek across the pestilential Isthmus of Panama. Before the gold strike, only four vessels arrived in San Francisco from the East Coast in a year. In 1849, 775 vessels brought 91,000 people.

The clippers, generally built of soft woods, were extremely slender. Their beams were only about one-sixth of the length, and they flew extensive spreads of sail. They were capable of sailing in the wild winds around Cape Horn and up the west coast of South America. Some of these clippers set records on their maiden voyages and never equalled them. They were excellent investment for their owners, often recovering their full cost on the first trip, because of the amount of cargo they could carry and the inflated price it would bring to supply California's mushrooming population.

The great spurt in building clipper ships in America was concentrated in the decade

As the age of sail came to an end, shipbuilders took advantage of old and new technology. In 1878, when the wind was right, the 1608-ton **Agnes** *could rely on the same forces of nature that propelled cargo ships for centuries.*

1848 to 1858, but the clippers were fairly short-lived. Many of these soft wood ships lasted only five years before they became waterlogged and leaky. The Civil War, starting in 1861, produced a hiatus in clipper-building.

Meanwhile, England had a somewhat similar boom based on the discovery of gold in Australia in 1849. British ship owners chartered American ships and built clippers of their own. By that time, England had little oak left in her forests and had to import wood for shipbuilding. The British built all-wooden clippers using hardwoods until about 1863, and then turned to composite construction, with iron frames and teak planking. These composite clippers were usually smaller than the American clippers and never exceeded their records, but they were superior at sailing in light winds, and this suited their employment on the China run. American clippers dominated the job of hauling tea from China in about 1850, but by 1870, the British craft took over the work. The famous *Cutty Sark,* the only clipper still in existence, is an example of composite construction.

The U.S. clippers' China trade had a great impact on American taste and culture. Sea captains brought back great quantities of Chinese and other oriental paintings, silk, pottery and other objects of art, as well as products of the Pacific Islands that the clippers visited. These works of art from other cultures decorated the homes of captains and ship owners in New England and were frequently exhibited in their home towns. This influence is recorded in exhibits at the Peabody Museum at Salem, Massachusetts.

The clipper ships and earlier vessels had long, straight keels and used inside ballast. The full keel was a standard feature of ship design until a sloping keel, deeper at the stern than at the stem, was put on some schooners. The next step was to use outside ballast attached to the keel on yachts but not on larger vessels.

The advance of technology and the scarcity of suitable wood brought the next major development in sailing ships—the iron ship. The first iron clipper, built in Great Britain in 1870, was *Lord of the Isles.* The opening of the Suez Canal in 1869 gave steamships a great advantage in the China trade. The clippers had to turn to hauling lumber from Australia.

Photo by Mark Sexton, Peabody Museum of Salem

Many a Tall Ship has been lost at sea. Fortunately, the tales of heroic rescues are almost as popular.

The iron ship was soon followed by the steel ship—about 1885. At first glance, iron and steel sound like materials too heavy for sailing vessels. They are stronger than wood, however, and their weight is countered by the fact that iron hulls can be thinner than wooden ones.

After the clipper ships, the next development in cargo-carrying vessels was the construction of larger ships. While the clippers emphasized speed and had limited cargo-hauling ability because of their slender hulls, the later ships emphasized capacity, and changed to wide hulls like those of the steamships that were their competitors.

These larger ships, over 190 feet in length, were built mainly in New England and were known as down-Easters. They were built during the slow recovery of shipbuilding after the Civil War. These ships carried relatively less sail than the highly canvassed clippers, but were nearly as fast because of their greater length and ability to carry sail in high winds.

The hefty windjammers, full-rigged ships and barks, continued to carry freight wherever they could, and one run they found profitable was the hauling of nitrates from Chile. The opening of the Panama Canal in 1914 ruined that business for sailing vessels, as it provided a great short-cut for the steamships. Non-perishable bulk cargo such as lumber, coal and steel rails was hauled by sailing ships well into the present century. One of the last of these great ships was *Herzogin Cecilie,* a four-masted bark built in 1902 and lost in 1936.

The last great fleet of deepwater, square-rigged sailing vessels was the famous Erikson fleet, based at Mariehamn, in the Aland Islands, off the coast of Finland. In the 1920's and 1930's, Captain Gustaf Erikson owned 20 steel windjammers that he bought when others gave up the attempt to compete with steamships. Erikson found work for his ships in hauling grain from South Australia to England, even though he had to send his ships south without cargo and could make only one round trip a year. He also scratched up some profit by taking on passengers and charging cadets for sail training aboard his ships.

World War II ended what little was left of his business, and Erikson died in 1947. However, several of his ships remain as museums. There are three in the United States: *Star of India* at San Diego, *Balclutha* at San Francisco, and *Moshulu* at Philadelphia.

At about the same period in this century when the great trading vessels could no longer make a profit under sail, the schooners engaged in fishing for cod on the Grand Banks also came to the ends of their careers. Many of these schooners were built at Gloucester, Massachusetts, or other ports in New England. There were driven from the sea by ships with engines.

Some glorious examples of square-rigged ships and schooners survive now as sail training vessels, and they may be seen whenever the Tall Ships gather.

They built them strong and they built them fast. The clipper **Glory of the Seas,** *designed by Donald McKay, was constructed in East Boston in 1869.* Peabody Museum of Salem

Shipboard life had its quiet moments. Boys took time from hard chores aboard **Cutty Sark** *in the 1870s.* Peabody Museum of Salem

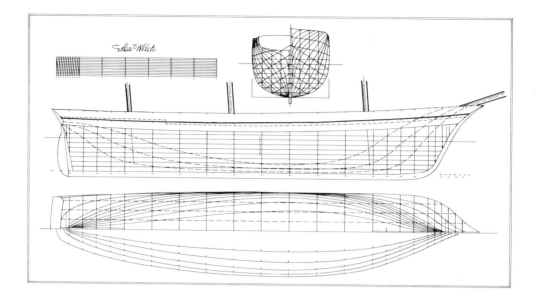

The Lines of The Hull

Gradual changes in the design and construction methods used for Tall Ships are reflected in the shape of the hulls. These changes are often difficult to express in words, and are best depicted by naval architects' drawings and accurate models.

The "lines" of *Sea Witch* illustrate how well a hull is shaped. One outline shows the sheerline at the top, the shape of the bow, stern and rudder, and the shape of the bottom, including the keel. Curved lines indicate the shape of the hull in the same way that a topographical map shows hills and valleys. In a boat with a blunt bow, the lines from the bow flowing down toward the bottom will be close together, while those for a boat with a more pointed bow will be far apart. Similarly, the lines near the bottom, indicating its shape, will be close together if the bottom is nearly flat and further apart if it slopes up gradually or is more rounded.

The view from the bottom, looking up from under the boat, shows only half the hull since both halves will be the same. The profile accurately shows the shape of the boat; whether it is slender or beamy can be seen at a glance as the eye compares the width to the length.

A third drawing shows the ends of the boat—views from the bow and stern. A clear picture of the beam can be seen from these perspectives—the way the topsides are shaped as they go down from the sheerline to the waterline and on to the bottom, and how the boat is shaped at each end. The transom, if there is any, shows on the view from the stern.

While there are not a great many different rigs, there are many ways the hull of a boat or ship can be shaped. Over the centuries ship designers have figured out good designs for vessels created to accomplish different tasks, and changes in hull shapes have evolved gradually.

Sailboat design has not reached perfection: naval architects are still struggling to find ways to design yachts that will go a little faster, will be more seaworthy, or more comfortable; usually they can deliver only one of those qualities without sacrificing some measure of the others. It is well to remember when admiring the Tall Ships that each may have been a great design in its day, but each depended on the success of the long procession of designs that preceded it and the naval architects who drew them were standing on the shoulders of generations of earlier designers.

In stories about the clipper ships, many of which are unduly romanticized, much has been written about the genius of Donald McKay, designer and builder of *Sovereign of the Seas* and many other excellent clippers. He was not alone. Nathaniel B. Palmer, successful as both a ship captain and a designer, designed *Samuel Russell* and other clippers. John W. Griffiths, the first American naval architect, designed *Rainbow* and *Sea Witch,* often considered the greatest of the clippers. Another gifted man, Samuel H. Pook, designed *Surprise* and *Defiance.*

Navigation

Knowledge And Instruments

Early ships sailed on rivers or along coasts within sight of land, and in all probability traveled only by day. The first instrument for navigation was the lead line, with which the sailor tested the depth of the water to avoid running aground. The ocean was a great unknown.

Sometime during the first thousand years B.C., the Phoenicians learned that the North Star moves little in the sky, and could be used as a point of reference for figuring direction on the sea at night. They understood that when the sun was at its highest point in the sky from their viewpoint in the eastern Mediterranean, it was toward the south. They also used the wind rose, a circular card similar to a compass card, to relate the one known direction to all others.

The earliest known chart of the sea, from about 700 B.C., depicts the world as a disc. The idea that the earth is a sphere was first proposed by Pythagoras in 580 B.C. By the second century A.D., Ptolemy of Alexandria produced a map showing with remarkable accuracy the Mediterranean, the Red Sea and the Persian Gulf. The map also indicated the Canary Islands in the west and China in the east.

The compass was known in China as far back as 1100 B.C., and apparently the Vikings used a lodestone as a primitive compass as early as 868 A.D. Compasses were used by the time of Prince Henry the Navigator (1394-1460), but sailors at that time did not realize that there is a magnetic pole which made the north shown on the compass somewhat different from the north on a chart. Charts did exist then–drawn on sheepskins or goatskins and showing known coastlines. There were also collections of notes about rocks, shoals, anchorages and other details observed by seafarers. Prince Henry recruited astronomers and mathematicians who compiled the first reliable tables for determining latitude by measuring the altitude of the sun. This, in time, resulted in lines of latitude being added to Portuguese charts, which were regarded as the best in the 15th and 16th Centuries during the great age of exploration.

One of the earliest instruments for navigation was the astrolabe, invented in the 10th Century. It consists of a disc or ring with a sighting ruler pivoting at its center. The altitude of the sun or a star is sighted along the ruler, whose position on the perimeter gives the reading of altitude. From that information, latitude could be figured. Another simple early navigational instrument that works in the same way is the cross staff, or fore staff, invented in 1342. It consists of a horizontal straight piece of wood, with several movable vertical pieces sliding on it. The observer holds one end of the horizontal staff to his eye and adjusts one of the vertical pieces until its lower end is at the horizon and its upper end is in line with the sun or a selected star. Then he reads the altitude from the staff.

Converting a reading of altitude to a measurement of latitude is not difficult, although taking the reading on a pitching deck is far from easy. If one is observing the North Star from the North Pole, it will be overhead; that is, the angle as compared with the horizontal will be 90 degrees. At the other extreme, if one were at the equator, and saw the North Star, it would be on the horizon and the angle would be zero. If the angle, measured at another place, turned out to be 45 degrees, the observer would be halfway between the equator and the North Pole, at 45 degrees north latitude. Thus, with a primitive instrument, it was possible to get a rough approximation of latitude. On a small ship's pitching deck, it was difficult to use the cross staff or its successors, the octant and sextant. In 1731, John Hadley invented a reflecting octant, which used the arc of one-eighth of a circle. The arc was enlarged to one-sixth of a circle in the sextant, which followed in 1757.

Determining longitude is a different story. To figure longitude from observing celestial bodies, it is necessary to know the position they have reached above the earth. This requires knowing the time accurately and early navigators did not have accurate time pieces. Early clocks used the pendulum, but the rolling of ships upset the pendulum. The balance and the hairspring mechanism was invented in 1675, leading to the chronometer in 1759. That opened the way for a great advance in celestial navigation, since sailors could plot both latitude and longitude and know where they were on the oceans.

Marine charts showing coast lines and lights were improved in the 17th Century, and by the end of the 18th Century charts showed the various depths of water.

Knowledge of navigation was advanced in 1799 when Nathaniel Bowditch, an American mathemetician and astronomer, published what became the basic text in celestial navigation, *New American Practical Navigator*. It showed how to determine longitude and offered an improved mentod for calculating latitude. He also included mathematical tables and information on winds and currents. Now the book is referred to simply as "Bowditch" and is published by the U.S. government in two volumes.

Vital knowledge on winds and currents in the Atlantic, Pacific and Indian Oceans was published in the middle of the 19th Century by Matthew F. Maury, who obtained his information primarily from the logs of sailing vessels. Maury put together and added details to what experienced sea captains already knew about the specific routes they traveled–how to take advantage of prevailing winds to sail mainly downwind. They had to have that knowledge because all the the square-rigged sailing vessels were poor performers at sailing upwind, although they excelled at sailing before the wind or on a reach. They often had to wait for a fair wind. Heading upwind, they could not sail closer than 70 degrees from the wind direction. Modern fore-and-aft rigged sailboats can sail at 45 degrees or less from the wind direction.

The China Trade

A banker, Robert Morris, and a group of New York merchants were responsible for the building of the first ship for the United States-China trade. When *Empress of China* made her first trading voyage from Boston to Canton in 1784, her cargo consisted of otter and seal skins and 30 tons of ginseng root, because those were the only products that the Americans knew the Chinese would accept in trade for the teas and silks the Americans wanted to bring back.

At that time, ginseng (*panax quinquefolium*) grew profusely in moist woodlands in New York and New England and was highly valued by the Chinese as a supposed aphrodisiac and heart stimulant. In the U.S., it has been popular periodically as a tonic and is therefore no longer so common in American woodlands. The name ginseng is a perversion of the Chinese Jim-chen, which translates to "man-like".

There either was not enough ginseng or the Chinese found it ineffective, so the search was on for other merchandise that would appeal to the Chinese. Otherwise, the teas, silks, nankeen and porcelain would have to be paid for in gold and silver coin. New Englanders, in vessels about 100 feet long, developed one answer: the Northwest-Hawaii-China triangle, which involved an 11-month outward voyage with trade stops along the way.

In 1787, two vessels, *Columbia* and *Washington*, laden with iron tools, looking-glasses and assorted novelties, sailed from Boston, around Cape Horn and up the northwest coast to trade with American Indians for sea otter skins, which Chinese mandarins prized. In Hawaii, the China-bound vessels would pick up sandalwood and sail to Canton. Incidentally, in 1792, *Columbia* stretched American exploration by sailing into the mouth of her namesake river, establishing United States' claim to the Oregon country. *Columbia* was also the first American ship to circumnavigate the globe.

Merchant ship captains from Salem, Massachusetts, had a different approach to China; they took advantage of the prevailing winds and the monsoon seasons by sailing eastward around the Cape of Good Hope. In this way, they added India and Indonesia to their trading routes. By the turn of the 18th Century they were literally giving Boston, New York and Philadelphia based ships a run for their money.

The most remunerative, if unscrupulous, trade was in opium. Opium was illegal in China but very popular there, and able to be smuggled profitably. The only American shipping firm that did not partake of this easy money was nicknamed "Zion's Corner". This opium trade, the opium war of 1839-42, and the subsequent opening of more Chinese ports and products spurred on the American design and building of more capacious but speedier ships, known as China "clippers". With the speed of their new vessels, American merchant captains were able to deliver tea, that perennial English favorite, from China to London faster than English ships could get that cargo home.

From the earliest days of American-China trade, when the rulers of China regulated trade severely by prohibiting any foreigners from entering the mainland, American merchant ship captains dealt with the Co-Hong, a group of Chinese merchants, at special factory-warehouse settlements along the Pearl River outside the gates of Canton. Apparently there was a good relationship among the traders, who were well-educated men, eager to find ways to please the new merchants.

Interestingly, America's first China clipper, launched in 1844 in response to the expanded China market was named *Houqua*, to honor the Canton merchants' leader whom the American captains respected highly.

On the Seamy Side of Sailing Ships

Working on sailing vessels of the 18th and 19th Centuries was not easy. It had many degrading and despicable aspects in addition to the wormy food, cramped and ill-ventilated quarters, and the hard labor that seamen endured.

With widespread willingness to disobey laws and to ignore common decency, shipowners' greed was often clear. During Colonial days in America, smuggling was common and piracy was rampant. Indeed, pursuing those occupations was among the major incentives for developing speed in American sailing vessels.

Another activity in which fortunes were made with total disregard for human rights was the slave trade. In the early 18th Century, this trade was thriving and was so developed that a triangular route was followed to make the most efficient use of cargo space on all three legs of a voyage. Ships from New England hauled rum to Africa where they bartered it for black people already enslaved along the West coast. There, lumber brought from home was used to build a new deck between the main deck and cargo deck. Often with only three feet of headroom, slaves were put in chains and shipped to the West Indies, where they were sold along with the lumber that had been the temporary deck. Then the ship was loaded with molasses and sugar to be hauled home for making rum.

Another profitable practice was the traffic in coolies. Coolies were extremely low-paid workers brought from China, treated as slaves and forced to work at the unhealthy and detestable task of digging guano and loading it onto ships from the Chinchas, three small islands near the coast of Peru. During a few years in the late 1850's, too many clippers were built for existing trade routes, and many clipper owners sent their vessels into the coolie and guano trade to keep their ships working profitably.

Hauling the coolies was, of course, a dishonorable business. Workers were supposed to be employed near Peru for five years, with decent working conditions. Instead, they were underfed and brutally forced to work seven days a week. Few lasted the five years. Many died from starvation or from breathing guano dust; many committed suicide by throwing themselves off the island's cliffs.

Coolies were hauled to Australia in addition to Peru. The clipper owners received $50 to $80 a head for shipping coolies. By packing in 800 workers, the ship could earn at least $40,000 for a single consignment of human cargo. In 1857, the governments of the United States and Britain outlawed the use of their ships for such trade. The business did not end without a profit, however. Peru bought American clippers and continued carrying workers from foreign shores.

Hauling guano was undoubtedly the most nauseating job that American sailing vessels undertook. The reeking yellow dust of guano, the excrement from birds and animals (in this case, seals) used to fertilize farms, penetrated everything on the ships. It was a worse form of physical pollution than the vile odors emanating from the try-pots of whaling ships. On the Chinchas, guano in some spots was 150 feet deep.

The Opium War, a one-sided aggression in which Great Britain defeated the virtually defenseless Chinese, was another example of misuse of Tall Ships. Before the war was fought from 1839 to 1842, English and American ships were smuggling opium into China. That cargo was illegal but very popular. The British grew the opium poppies in India, the Americans purchased opium in Turkey, and both found an illicit market in China. When the Chinese emperor clamped down on the smuggling and forced British ships to hand over a huge quantity of the drug, valued at $12 million, the British government was outraged.

Overlooking the illegality of the opium trade, the British used the confiscation of that cargo as an excuse to make war on China. They burned the flimsy wooden junks and slaughtered thousands of Chinese.

The price of ending the war, the treaty of Nanking, was high for China. It included allowing England to occupy the island of Hong Kong. The British continued to smuggle opium, using Hong Kong as a convenient base of operations. In 1844, the United States managed to negotiate for itself access to more ports in China. That opened the way for expanded trade in the Orient and allowed the opium traffic to prosper more easily than before.

Significant Dates in the History of Sail

580 B.C.	Pythagoras stated the earth is a sphere.
150 B.C.	Hipparchus invented the astrolabe.
130 A.D.	Ptolemy showed how to depict a curved surface on a flat chart.
1078 A.D.	The *cinque ports* were established. Five ports on the south coast of England were given special privileges by the king, in return for naval protection.
1206	Press gangs were legalized for manning England's royal ships.
1483	Alphonsine Tables, the first astronomical tables, were published in Spain.
1536	*Mary Rose,* built in 1510, was armed with heavy guns and became the first ocean-going warship with big guns inside her hull.
1569	Gerard Mercator invented the Mercator projection, representing the globe as a cylinder for mapmaking.
1608	The marine telescope was invented.
1628	Sweden's great wooden warship *Vasa* sank on her maiden voyage.
1675	The Greenwich Observatory was established in Greenwich, England.
1718	Edward Teach, the pirate known as Blackbeard, was killed. The days of both piracy and privateering were nearing their end.
1731	Hadley's octant, a forerunner of the sextant, was invented.
1757	Campbell developed the sextant, improving the octant.
1759	John Harrison invented the chronometer.
1799	Bowditch published *New American Practical Navigator*.
1818	The first regularly scheduled service for passengers, freight and mail between New York and Liverpool started Jan. 15, by the Black Ball Line.
1819	The first steamer crossed the Atlantic: *Savannah,* with paddle wheels and auxiliary sails.
1838	The first ship under steam alone crossed the Atlantic: *Sirius*.
1851	*Flying Cloud* sailed from New York to San Francisco in 89 days, 21 hours setting a record.
1854	*Flying Cloud* beat that record, completing the trip in 89 days, 8 hours.
1854	*Champion of the Seas* sailed 465 nautical miles in one day—a record for sailing vessels.
1855	Matthew F. Maury charted ocean winds and currents in his *Physical Geography of the Sea*.
1859	Oil was discovered in Pennsylvania—the beginning of the end for whaling.
1869	Suez Canal opened.
1895-1898	Captain Joshua Slocum became the first person to sail around the world alone.
1902	First wireless message was sent across the Atlantic.
1914	Panama Canal opened.

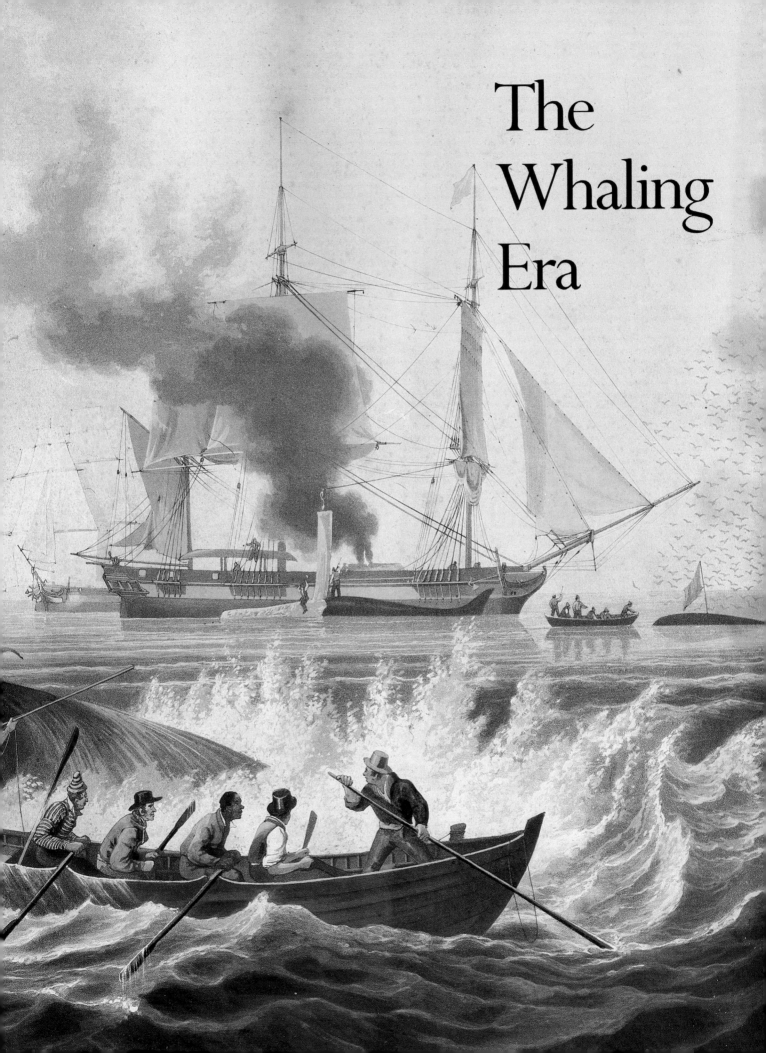

The
Whaling
Era

Whaling

The sea itself has been a challenge to humans, and the largest denizens of the oceans added another challenge. Men in small boats and large have faced the double challenge of pursuing whales on the seas of the world. In America, the first whalers were the Native Americans, who used wooden spears, operating from canoes, to attack whales that came close to the shore. They taught the early colonists their method with right whales.

The first concentrations of whaling activity by the colonists were on the south shore of Long Island and on the islands of Martha's Vineyard and Nantucket, starting in the 1670's. Those early whale hunters used small wooden boats to pursue whales they had seen from shore, and when they succeeded in killing a whale, they towed it home to cut it up and cook the blubber on the beach. The stench of the rendering process is probably the first example of industrial air pollution in America. There were complaints and even restrictions, but there was money in whale oil, which made excellent fuel for lamps and was used as a lubricant.

Before long, the colonists realized they could catch more—and different—whales by going out to sea after them, rather than pursuing only those right whales that came inshore to feed. Gradually, the whalers took their rendering equipment—their "try-pots"—with them on their ships, and made whaling an offshore industry. Whaling had become big business by the time of the American Revolution; there were about 150 whaling ships based at Nantucket, with scores more based on nearby Martha's Vineyard, Long Island and Cape Cod. The power of the British Navy ruined American whaling during the American Revolution by destroying the ships. Colonists had to return to using tallow candles made from the fatty tissues of land animals to illuminate their houses instead of lamps fueled by oil from whale blubber.

Whaling revived after the Revolution, only to be interrupted again in the War of 1812 and revived a second time when that war ended. Then came the greatest prosperity ever experienced by American whalemen. Lubricants were needed for new machinery being introduced, whalebone was in demand for use in corsets,

Whaling scene showing an American ship. Watercolor by A.L. Morel-Fatio, 1842

whips and umbrellas, and there was a good market for spermaceti candles. New Bedford became the greatest whaling port in the world, with about half the American fleet.

The whaling vessels perfected in the 19th Century were not triumphs of grace or beauty, but of utility for the dirty work conducted on them and from them. They had to be large and broad to carry whale boats and have room for the hundreds of barrels of whale oil they brought home in their holds. Heavily built and ready to go anywhere, they were designed for hauling men and cargo, not for speed.

They did sail almost anywhere, though. Wintering in Honolulu, San Francisco or the Western Pacific, chasing the gray whales along the West coast of North America, sailing north through Bering Strait in pursuit of bowhead whales, some of these seagoing oil factories even ventured into the Antarctic.

When a whale was sighted by lookouts at the mastheads, the seamen quickly launched the whaleboats. In contrast to the ships, the boats were slender, light craft of about 30 feet, loaded with equipment but still able to carry six men. They would row close to the quarry so that the man at the bow could plunge a harpoon into the whale, attaching the boat to it with a strong, 300-foot line. If the men were lucky, the whale would submerge for a time and then come back to surface and the mate would thrust in a six-foot lance for the kill. If they were unlucky, the whale would haul the boatload of whalemen on what they called a "Nantucket sleighride" until the creature was thoroughly tired and the mate could give the whale that death-dealing lance stabbing. At worst, a mighty whale could easily smash the whaleboat or even sink the ship.

Once the dangerous chase was over, the really repulsive and difficult labor of whaling began—the conversion of a few thousand pounds of bleeding, slithery whale to the wealth that would make the whole procedure worth the mess. The whale was towed to the ship and lashed there while the blubber was stripped off and cut into "blanket pieces." These were hoisted onto the ship and down a hatch amidships to what some whalemen called "the reception room." In stinking swelter, the blubber was cut into smaller pieces and cooked in large iron try-pots to render the oil. Those pots held about 300 gallons; a very large whale might yield that much.

Meanwhile, the rest of the whale, in sections, would be on the deck with all available hands helping extract whatever was of value. Whale meat, blood and grease covered the deck and added equally nauseating stench to the output of the foul-smelling try-pots. The oil had to be lifted into a copper tank for cooling and then poured into barrels freshly made by the ship's cooper. Then the barrels had to be hauled below for storage. Everyone, from captain to cabin boy, worked day and night from the moment a whale was sighted until the processing was completed. If there were many whales in the area, as many as possible would be killed, until the ship could hold no more oil or the whales had moved to safer seas. It was all around-the-clock hard labor, in a filthy place.

There was little or no rest for the weary whaling crew. The men were put to work cleaning up the slimy scum that seemed to reach all surfaces of the ship—another dreadful job. They scrubbed everything with a mixture of lye and saltwater, effective for removing dirt but no respecter of the skin on seamen's hands. After that, all the men and the clothing they wore during the whale-processing needed to be washed. For this job, saltwater and urine were mixed to loosen the dirt for later scrubbing.

No wages or salary was paid. Everyone shared in the whaling profits, in very unequal portions, with the captain/shipowner getting the largest and the cabin boy the least. Sometimes after a not very profitable voyage the seaman would end up owing money, having used up his credit in purchases from the ship's stores. In any case, once on a whaling ship, everyone would want to capture as many whales as possible so the voyage could be shortened.

Mealtimes did not brighten the life of the residents of the forecastle, for their food was minimal and often wormy. Their regular fare consisted of salt beef or pork, baked beans or pea soup, served with an inferior bread called "hard tack." There was coffee with molasses and duff for a special Sunday dessert. This was a boiled flour pudding, sometimes with raisins. The delicacy got its name from a ship's cook's

The pictures of the whaling era are fading now, but the images of the hard labor remain. This late 19th Century photo shows whalemen cutting the blanket of blubber and hoisting it aboard a vessel in the Pacific.

translation of a recipe for dough pudding. According to him, dough rhymed with tough and rough. The name stuck through the centuries.

The living conditions of the whaling seamen were no better than their food. They were crammed into small bunks in the low-ceilinged forecastle, with little ventilation, no privacy and no room for personal belongings except in their sea chests. Wet clothing and gear was draped on hooks wherever there was space for a hook, accentuating the fetid atmosphere. When there were no whales there were always sails that needed tending or repairing. When there was free time, whalemen worked at scrimshaw, a craft that was born in the forecastle. They carved and constructed many ingenious objects from the whalebone or baleen, such as decorative combs for sweethearts' hair, crimpers for pie crust, or yarn-winders. Examples of this primitive art can now be found in many coastal museums. Erractic mail delivery was one of the tribulations faced by those aboard whaling ships. Ship captains would frequently change their plans if they learned from other whaleships that a plentiful supply of whales could be found in a different direction, so letters from home could be addressed only to the ship by name, not location.

When ships met at sea, one of the best features of a gamming session was the exchange of letters—homebound mail put on a homeward ship, mail for an outbound ship passed on to the captain whose ship was headed that way. Because of the ad lib nature of the pursuit of whales, sometimes letters passed back and forth from ship to ship for years. Six months for a letter from home was considered prompt delivery! One captain's wife reported that she sent 100 letters to her husband during his three-year voyage; he received only six.

In the mid 1850's, a postoffice was established in Honolulu, which was then a popular whaling center during the winter months. There were informal mail drops on some uninhabited islands, the most ingenious one in the Galapagos, on Charles Island. Affixed to the top of a post at the head of a sheltered cove was a large box covered with a giant tortoise shell. Whalemen called this location Post Office Bay. Outward bound whalers would leave mail from New England for whaleships already in the Pacific. Ships whaling the area would pick up letters and drop off others to be collected later by homeward bound whalers.

In 1859, petroleum was discovered in Pennsylvania. Eventually, one of its derivatives, kerosene, superceded whale oil for use in lamps. But long before that happened, the Civil War resulted in the loss of about half the American whaling fleet.

After the Civil War the industry revived yet again, but whales had become more scarce because of the ruthless zeal of whale hunters over the years. After hunting the right whales almost to extinction and pursuing sperm whales throughout the Pacific and Indian Oceans, the whalers expanded their year-round itinerary to include Arctic waters.

In the late 1840's it was discovered that bowhead whales existed in great numbers in the Sea of Okhotsk, off the coast of Siberia, so that became a favorite whaling site. Whalers penetrated farther into the Arctic for an even greater supply of the new wealth of bowheads. Ruled by the promise of dollars and a total disregard for the future, they killed the bowheads, removed the baleen and discarded the rest of the creatures. Why? Because equipping a ship for processing the blubber and extracting oil was expensive, messy and time-consuming, and oil would bring only 30 cents a pound. Baleen was easier to get and was worth four dollars a pound. As a result of their profligacy, the whalers found the bowheads gone from the whaling scene in little more than 25 years.

Enthusiasm for Arctic whaling must have also been tempered by the experience of the 33 whaleships that lingered too late in their northern hunt in 1871. The crews had to abandon their ships, oil and all, when the ice closed them in completely. The heavily-laden ships were left there, but the people aboard were rescued by seven ships that had retreated southward to the open seas. Risking their valuable cargo and the lives of their crews because of increasing cold, the rescue ships managed to fit all the Arctic survivors aboard and take them home to the safety of San Francisco.

Eventually, most whalers began pursuing gray whales along the West coast of North America, at the same time many ship owners shifted their base of operations to the more convenient San Francisco. By 1895, the gray whales, too, had all but disappeared.

Looking back on the history of whaling, it is not difficult to isolate the incentive that drove men to risk the dangers and endure the hardships. It was the profit motive. Shipowners could make fortunes in whaling. Some vessels made enormous profits year after year. An unusually high return was realized by *Lagoda*, which cost about $5,000 to build and earned more than $650,000 in 12 years. In 1846 there were at least 70,000 men working on whaling ships. They brought home $70 million worth of whale oil and other products of their labor.

Whaling today often involves much more wholesome pursuits. While Americans of the previous two centuries were interested only in killing the whales, the main emphasis now is on saving this cetacean mammal from any further threat of extinction. In the United States and internationally, research teams gather data on the whale population, tracking them to learn more about their habits and behavior.

"Save the Whale" activists have formed many organizations, including Greenpeace, which wages a direct-action, nonviolent campaign to stop whale hunting anywhere in the world. Earthwatch, another conservation group, is a New England-based enterprise that trains interested young people to join expeditions to the Pacific and the Caribbean to help record observations of the humpback whales.

On the U.S. Pacific coast, ships take enthusiastic passengers on cruises to see migrating whales. Similar short cruises are becoming more popular on the East coast, where museums and land-based conservation centers help educate more people each year about the importance of protecting these great sea mammals. One thing is certain—on these whale-watching cruises any cry of "Whale off!" or "There's a blow!" is guaranteed to evoke a fast display of cameras rather than harpoons.

Deck space was at a premium on many whalers.

The Peabody Museum of Salem

The docks of New Bedford were still booming in 1870, as thousands of barrels of whale oil awaited shipment to eager customers throughout New England.

In 1865, Merrill's Wharf in New Bedford was busy receiving the bountiful harvest of the whaling trade.

Women and the Sea

Women as Pirates
Aboard Whaling Ships
Wives of Merchant Ship Captains
Heroines at Sea

Lowell Lytle

Women and the Sea

Where were the women in the story of sailing ships through the ages? Do we have to be satisfied with the myths, the legends, the tales of blessing and curses? Beyond Greek mythology's Amphitrite, Thetis, Galatea and the 47 other Nereids, those nymphs who danced and sang across the seas and rescued mariners in distress, and all the other mythic females—where were the women?

Of course, women have traveled on ships for centuries as figureheads, under the bowsprit, where their bare-breasted beauty was thought to calm raging storms. Every ship is a "she," and the sea itself is personified as a woman. Sea chanteys that sailors sang to help the rhythm of anchor-hauling and sail-hoisting often referred to women. The ritual of ship-christening at launching is still a woman's job.

Richard Henry Dana wrote about the custom of hanging a length of rope over the side of a ship on a homeward voyage, to be used by wives and sweethearts of crew members to pull the ship home with magical speed born of their yearning for their men. Dana said that when there was a favorable wind on a homeward trip, it was customary for the report at the change of watch to include: "The Boston girls have had hold of the tow-rope all the watch."

Contrary to popular belief, there were women aboard ships, often disguised as men. Records of these women are paltry since their real names would not appear on any ship's muster list. If their sex was discovered, they were usually removed from the ship as soon as a port could be reached.

Almost incredibly, the gender of these women was rarely discovered by other sailors. Wearing heavy corseting and having their breasts tightly bound, they suffered years of hard work and abuse.

Some of the women served on both British and American warships; some became pirates, even commanding pirate ships as far back as the 16th Century.

Others were the staunch wives of whaling captains who chose to go to sea with their husbands rather than be left at home for the duration of those long voyages. Wives of merchant ship captains shared more spacious quarters with their husbands and made the most of their far-flung travels. Occasionally, women married to captains of the handsome, speedy clippers sailed with their husbands. Some of the most interesting stories of women on ships came from the wives of shipowners and captains, through the journals they kept.

Here are the stories of a few unusual women among the many who sailed on ships from the time of Queen Elizabeth to the great days of sailing when clippers were in their glory.

Women as Pirates

Grace O'Malley

A rich veneer of Irish legend colors the story of Grace O'Malley. Beneath that veneer is the hard fact that she was the daughter of well-to-do pirates and inherited the leadership of a very successful pirate fleet. She was born on Clare Island off the coast of Ireland and became a sailor at an early age as a member of her father's crew.

Before going to sea, Grace was a land-based marauder. As a small girl, she climbed a cliff near her home where eagles suspected of killing the family's sheep had their nest. Grace reached the nest and killed the birds but she carried the ugly scar of an eagle's talons on her forehead for the rest of her life.

Grace was trained in seamanship and piracy by her father, and she was his heir. She and her band preyed on shipping between Cork and ports in Spain and Portugal, both of which had large fleets of ships in the 16th Century. Grace was so disruptive of commerce that Queen Elizabeth offered a reward for her capture, but the pirate eluded all pursuers. Later, however, she made peace with the queen, who needed powerful allies. By one account, Queen Elizabeth actually knighted one of Grace O'Malley's sons.

Another tale, possibly far-fetched, tells of an encounter with a Spanish ship when Grace was gray-haired but still in charge. The Spaniards boarded her ship, but Grace faced them on deck with a pistol in her right hand and a sword in her left, with her long gray hair flying in the breeze and the eagle talons' scar burning brightly on her flushed brow. The Spaniards took her for a fiend with supernatural powers and immediately retreated.

One thing is certain about Grace O'Malley: her first name was ill-chosen.

Hsi Kai Ching Yih

The Chinese entered piracy in the Pacific at the end of the 18th Century with a kind of "Robin Hood" enterprise. On the southern coast of China, severe flooding had destroyed the crops. People were starving while heavily laden merchant ships from England and other countries could be seen offshore. When one of the vessels was wrecked, coastal farmers and fishermen went out in small boats. expecting to salvage whatever was edible. When they found survivors guarding the sinking ship, they attacked and dispatched them quickly and took the food cargo back to their hungry villagers. These acts of desperation became a habit; piracy became a way of life for many China Coast fishermen.

The man who organized the pirates and consolidated their efforts was Captain Ching Yih, a formidable fighter. He built his pirate organization from one small junk and a 12-man crew to a sizable, disciplined fleet that became such a threat to shipping that the emperor once sent 40 ships to destroy his fleet. After Ching Yih had captured all 40 ships, he decided to add a wife to his life, and chose Hsi Kai from a group of slaves who were part of the prize from a recent raid. Far from docile, this beatiful woman insisted on being made co-commander of her husband's pirate armada. She filled the position dramatically, establishing herself as an awesome leader. When her husband died, she donned his uniform—a splendid robe of blue with gold embroidery—wore his helmet and swords, and took over leadership of the pirate empire with not a word of dispute from the pirate captains.

Apparently, Hsi Kai Ching Yih was much more organized and businesslike than most other pirates, keeping close control over the behavior of pirates in her fleet. Her regulations included many restrictive rules about the treatment of women. Posted aboard every boat in the pirate armada was an edict which included: "To use violence against any woman or to wed her without her permission shall be punished with death."

In addition to championing women's rights, this pirate queen kept a firm hold on the purse strings and the loot that was stored in a huge warehouse, to be shared by all. Special written permission had to be granted before any pirate could make a withdrawal of any of the booty.

Hsi Kai built up her many-squadroned fleet to almost 2,000 ships and more than 50,000 pirates. It was not defeat that ended Hsi Kai's pirate life, but an offer from the emperor of China that she couldn't resist. Her price for peace from piracy was complete amnesty, command of part of the imperial fleet and a palace. There she retired with her second husband, to have four children and grow old gracefully as a smuggler, ending the piracy that had constantly threatened the China Seas.

Lady Killegrew

There is a thin line between piracy and privateering. Piracy is the act of attacking ships, making off with whatever cargo of value they contain, and capturing or destroying the ship. It is, of course, illegal. Privateering involves the same acts and often the same indiciduals, employed by their government to attack and destroy enemy ships in time of war. This is patriotic endeavor. For hundreds of years, it was customary for countries to wink at piracy among their own people, knowing they'd come in handy as privateers when needed.

During the reign of Queen Elizabeth I, a titled Cornish couple had a prosperous career in piracy while enjoying the protection of the Crown. Lady Killigrew came from a family long involved in piracy, and her husband, Sir John, was the leader of an extensive network of pirates all around the coast of Great Britain. At the same time, like the fox guarding the chicken yard, Sir John was Vice-Admiral of Cornwall, Royal Governor of Pendennis Castle, and President of the Commissioners for Piracy.

The Killigrews plundered in peace for many years, never colliding with the law. Then greed, or an adventurous spirit, led Lady Killigrew in 1582 to undertake a foolhardly marauding mission. With a small boat and crew, she attacked a German ship lying peacefully at anchor in Falmouth harbor. She and her band murdered all the crew and helped themselves to the cargo, which included two barrels of weighty silver coins, and other valuables. That cargo turned out to have a very high price, however. Queen Elizabeth took a dim view of Lady K.'s ferocious escapade. The titled pirate and two of her crewmen were tried, convicted and sentenced to hang. For the two men, the hanging took place; the Queen had second thoughts about the value of the Cornish Lady, perhaps realizing how important her privateering services might be in the future. Lady Killigrew's sentence was commuted to a term in prison.

Going to California? The advertising for clipper ships pictured women as part of their sales pitch. But not all women were content merely to be passengers. As captains' wives, some were famous for heroic leadership.

SUTTON & CO'S

DISPATCH LINE FOR SAN FRANCISCO

Lowest Rates and no Detention.

POPULAR LINE—MAGNIFICENT SHIPS.

CLIPPER OF

SATURDAY, 6th November.

COLSON

BOSIO   ALBONI   LAGRANGE

The Splendid A 1 First-Class Clipper Ship

PRIMA DONNA

JOHN S. PRAY, Master,

IS RECEIVING HER CARGO AT PIER 10 E. R.

And will promptly sail as above.

This splendid Clipper was built expressly for the California trade, with the view to great speed, and the good delivery of Cargo. Stands A 1 extra, and very desirable to Shippers wishing to insure their own Goods. She is of moderate and convenient size, and takes her stand at once in the first rank of favorite Clippers.

SUTTON & CO., 58 South St., cor. Wall.

N. B.—We beg to inform our Shippers, that we pay particular attention to the Stowage and ventilation of all our vessels, and with first-class Clippers—low rates of Freight, and our usual prompt dispatch, present a most popular line to San Francisco.

NESBITT & CO., PRINTERS.

Photo by Mark Sexton, Peabody Museum of Salem

Women Aboard Whaling Ships

Unappealing as life aboard a whaling ship seems to our 20th Century senses, to the wife of a 19th Century whaling captain it was more inviting than the prospect of three to five fearful years of loneliness ashore, waiting for her husband to return from unknown oceans. Even more frightening, she didn't know whether he would return. Mail was a haphazard matter, and the report of a ship's disaster might take years to reach her. Also, there were tales of the beguiling life in the South Pacific that might ensnare a bewitched sea captain for years.

For these reasons, many New England women packed themselves, their children, their favorite household furnishings and their Bibles and went off to sea. They didn't go for love of the sea and certainly not to advance "women's rights". They went, quite simply, to make a home on a ship with their husbands. Along with their trunks and chests, they transferred their social values as well as their homemaking and nurturing talents from land to sea.

Most of these women had no problems with their roles. They expected to obey the captain, were pleased to be with him and make his life as much like New England as was possible on a 125-foot or longer workship. In the process of becoming a seafarer, a captain's wife brought a nurturing influence to the whaleship. In addition to caring for her children, she was concerned for the ship's crew. Since the ship wandered the oceans for years before returning home with its whale-wealth, there was time for a "family feeling" to develop, and mothering was a welcome addition.

A captain's wife usually had a mellowing influence on her husband's behavior, and although there was always punishment for misbehaving crew members, it was generally less harsh on a "lady ship".

Most of these Victorian women were quite religious, so it was natural for them to be concerned with the spiritual life of the crew. They prayed for the recovery of injured or sick seamen, for the conversion of any backsliders and for the safety of the voyage. Sometimes they conducted Sunday services and handed out bibles.

More practically, the women were willing and resourceful in medical emergencies, ready to hold a child or even a whaleman while the captain, as ship's doctor, performed primitive surgery.

Although some wives of whaling captains learned something about navigation, most of them continued their housewifely regimen: sewing, embroidering, caring for and teaching their children (and sometimes the cabin boy, who doubled as baby-sitter). Mending the captain's clothing was another regular occupation, and some women who had brought sewing machines aboard would mend a sail or even make a new one. It was also common practice for the captain's wife to raise chickens and pigs, which were a great enrichment to the captain's table. Writing in their journals occupied much of the women's leisure time. In fact, it is from such records that more has been learned about day-to-day whaling ship life than from the terse, factual entries in a captain's log.

Cooking was the responsibility of the steward and cook, but many women baked pies, cakes, cookies and special dessert treats, with the steward cleaning up. Birthdays and holidays were celebrated festively, weather and whales permitting. Handwashing, starching and ironing their voluminous skirts, petticoats, dresses and their fussy blouses could also have been done by the steward, but most women preferred to do those chores themselves. None of those jobs could have been easy. Waiting for a suitable washday might take weeks, and clothes hung out on deck in a brisk wind might be shredded before they were dried. Several days of fog and mist could get clothes mildewed instead of dry. Ironing, which involved having to lift weight on and off a hot stove constantly, sounds nightmarish. In spite of such difficulties, however, many shipboard wives recorded their pleasure at being with their husbands.

When there were whales, everything changed. All except the women were busy with the pursuit, killing and processing. For the women, this must have been an almost unbearably miserable time. Not only did they have to endure the hideous stench and filth that was part of the whale work, but they had to do everything for themselves. Since the steward, cook and cabin boy were engrossed in grease, the wives were left with total care of the children, keeping them safely out of the gory slime. The only positive note was the joyful prospect of more barrels of whale oil in the ship's hold, which meant bringing the voyage closer to an end.

For the long periods when there were no whales to chase and process, there was the plague of boredom, made more deadly with the accompanying pangs of homesickness. The best cure for this, for the wives, was a good gamming session.

Gamming was a social custom among whaling ships. Captains, officers, wives and crew visited each other at sea. When two ships sailed near each other, the captain of one would "speak" the other ship. This meant maneuvering close so that the captains could converse. They would talk about weather, whales, news of other ships and then, usually, one of the captains would invite the other to come aboard for a gam. If only one ship had a woman aboard, the "lady ship" would be the receiving ship. There was an ingenious transport for the visiting woman, whose full-skirted clothing made a rope ladder impractical. She would be lowered into one of the whaleboats in a "gamming chair", often a remodeled barrel with a seat and a rope sling, and hoisted onto the other ship.

While the captains were gamming on one ship, the mates of both whalers would be on the other. The crew participated too; they would take turns, with half a crew joining the other for awhile, then changing places.

When women participated in a gam, they traded stories and treasures, recipes and even plants and pets. Actually gamming was originated by ship captains in the earliest years of around-the-globe whaling, to exchange observations and information about where whales were more plentiful and to compare notes on the best routes.

In the mid-19th Century the most extensive gam of all was on shore in Honolulu, where as many as 400 ships would be anchored at times. It was said that it was often possible to "walk from one end of the harbor to the other without getting your feet wet." What had been a village of grass huts when the first whaleships stopped there in the 18th Century had become a miniature, tropical New England town. As one whaling wife wrote in her journal, "I kept wondering if I'd died and gone to heaven."

Often, whaleships would anchor at Honolulu, transfer the oil from their ships to merchant ships on their way home and then return to more Pacific whaling. During the time the whaleship was being refitted for its next whale-hunt, it was customary for the women to move into boarding houses on shore. There they and their husbands would enjoy carefree, self-indulgent vacations that would have shocked them in New England. There were afternoon teas with old friends and acquaintances from home, croquet, shopping, horseback riding, picnics on the beach and concerts in the evenings.

Meanwhile, back in the New England seacoast towns, the women who did not go to sea were running things. These wives, widows and sisters of whaling captains kept the families' business accounts, paid the bills and found markets for the products the men brought back from their voyages. That might include all the whale-connected treasure: oil, baleen and ambergris, as well as assorted "curiousities"—carvings, sculpture, mementoes from the exotic ports the whaleships visited. All of this was in addition to taking care of their property and children.

Because of the high death rate among the whaling men and the number of men making longer and longer voyages, the population of many seacoast towns was predominantly female. Although the women were in the majority, the laws of the time did not recognize them. They were responsible for the management of businesses and investments but they could not vote and had no political power. In Nantucket, toward the middle 1800's, women outnumbered men four to one, and the main streets of some towns were known as Petticoat Row because all the shops and business establishments were managed and owned by women.

Wives of Merchant Ship Captains

Since women in general were not found in the records of sailing ships of the 19th Century, unless they were related to the captain, one might assume that few females were knowledgeable enough to serve on a ship. It would be an incorrect assumption –navigation was taught in many New England schools, and girls as well as boys studied it. It was the attitude of the period, not the lack of interest or ability that kept individual women ashore. Unless as teenagers they successfully disguised themselves in male clothing and were able to "learn the ropes" as a cabin "boy," the only chance for a female was to be the wife or daughter of a sea captain.

For wives of captains of 19th Century merchant ships who accompanied their husbands to sea, shipboard living was much more pleasant than the whaling wives' experience. The difference between the two vessels was as great as the contrast between a foul-smelling factory and an elegant office suite, or between a sturdy, elderly truck and a handsome, new Cadillac. New England merchant ship captains were definitely Cadillac types.

Often, having started their sea-life as cabin boys, through years of hard work they were by now among the most affluent men in New England, along with doctors, lawyers and bankers. It was fitting that their ships should be as luxurious·as money and fine craftsmanship could make them. These captains were often owners or part-owners of the ships they commanded and were encouraged by their associates to take their wives along on trading voyages. A contented captain was less likely to linger in the warm islands of the Pacific, more committed to the purpose of the voyages: to make as much money for the owners as clever trading could assure, in the shortest time, to get back home with saleable cargo and prepare for the next voyage.

In general, the wives loved it. Of course, space on these ships was more restricted than their New England homes, but it was well-designed, and the captain's family had the best of it. Theirs was the after cabin; the area had skylights and was luxuriously appointed, with built-in furniture of handsome woods, ornately carved woodwork, gold leaf ornamentation, handcrafted lamps and sometimes stained glass windows in the main saloon. When the vessel was at rest in a port, oriental rugs would be brought out, along with silver tea sets and whatever could make the captain's leisure hours more homelike.

The family's food was the best that could be kept, with the limited means of preservation of pre-electric days, and the larder was replenished at each port with many more varieties of fresh fruits and vegetables than New England enjoyed. In general, meat was plentiful, salted for preservation. For the captain's wife, there was no servant problem: the steward, cook and cabin boy served the family.

If a baby was expected to be born on the voyage, a midwife would be likely to be aboard; if there were children, often a stewardess would also be on the ship. Usually, she was the wife of one of the officers and, in some cases, the stewardess would be paid as much as the first officer.

By the 1830's, it was said that the women from some coastal New England towns knew more about places across the seas than they knew about Boston. They were world travelers long before it was practicable to "see America first", and they weren't idle sightseers–they were traversing the oceans of the world for trade and profit.

For the children, as for everyone else aboard ship, life was disciplined, and there was no question about that. From books and journals written by people who sailed with their parents, their sea-going days were among their very happiest childhood memories.

This is easily believable if one thinks of the world geography those youngsters were learning about firsthand, with interested parents to share and enrich their new experiences. They visited exotic places where unknown kinds of plants and animals lived; they met and played with children who looked like no one they had ever seen, who spoke a language they could not understand, but with whom they could share games, giggles, toys and treasures. The New England children and their mothers would occasionally return to their ship with an unusual bird or small animal gift or carving, and always with their knowledge and curiosity about the world expanded.

While the ship was under way there were chores, as their part of keeping things shipshape. There were lessons, with textbooks from home and mother as teacher and supervisor. There were other lessons taught by their captain father—use of the compass, navigation, steering and the signal code flags. Both parents taught the need for order, quick response, immediate obedience. But it was the captain's wife who was responsible for keeping shipboard life running smoothly.

Playtime was necessarily quiet time, which made for some inventive games using pencil and paper or charts, card games using hand signals instead of speech. Reading was a popular pastime for the family, limited only by an often lean library. The imposed silence stemmed from the need for every officer to be able to sleep when he was not on watch, and somebody was always sleeping. That meant the only time for noisy exercise and play with tricycles, wagons and other "rolling stock" and the accompanying running, chatter and laughter was during the first "dogwatch", from four to six each afternoon. Dogwatch was a device used so that officers and crew would alternate the night shifts: those scheduled for four o'clock would be on duty for only two hours. Men coming off the normal four-hour watch at four p.m. would eat and rest for two hours and go on the second dog watch from six to eight p.m.

The captain, his wife and a companion onboard the Guy C. Goos, *a wood bark built in Bath, Maine, in 1879.*

Caroline Mayhew

Caroline Mayhew was the daughter of a Martha's Vineyard physician and the wife of whaling captain William Mayhew. Unlike most of the wives who went to sea, Mrs. Mayhew knew something about navigation. That and her knowledge about practical medicine, learned from her father, helped her save the lives of her husband and the crew of their bark, *Powhaton.* In 1846, a smallpox epidemic broke out on the ship, and Captain Mayhew was one of its victims, unable to continue the command. Caroline took over the navigation and command of *Powhaton* while nursing her husband and the stricken crew members. In the meantime, she fell ill with smallpox, too. Everyone aboard recovered, and the gratitude of the crew netted Caroline Mayhew a great collection of scrimshaw gifts of thanks.

The most unusual pet written about on any ship was Caroline Mayhew's kangaroo, a gift presented to her in New Zealand by some Maoris. The marsupial stayed with her on several voyages and returned with her to Martha's Vineyard where it became a favorite curiosity.

Mary Patten

The merchant marine of the 19th Century was surely a man's world. So it's enough to make one do a double take to see a woman's name on a hospital of the U.S. Merchant Marine Academy at King's Point, New York. But there it is: Mary Patten, honored for heroism and leadership in terrifying circumstances aboard a ship when she was only 19 years old. Her amazing exploit occurred in 1856, in a period when we think of women being busy at home while their men were off at sea.

There were, however, many instances where women married to clipper captains went to sea with their husbands and learned his profession. Such a woman was Mary Patten, who at the age of 16 was married to Joshua A. Patten, captain of the clipper *Neptune's Car.* On their first voyage together, she made herself generally useful and took lessons in navigation. An eager pupil, by the end of that voyage she knew how her husband ran the ship and how he found his way on the oceans.

In July, 1856, *Neptune's Car* and two other clippers set out for San Francisco. Clippers normally raced to build their reputations and future business. This voyage would take them around Cape Horn in winter, the most difficult time to undertake the hazardous passage. They had not gone far when Captain Patten discovered that his first mate was a saboteur who shortened sail when he was in charge and abused the crew. The first mate was put in irons. That meant the captain had to take over the first mate's normal watches because the second mate was ignorant of navigation and incapable of handling the ship. The long hours on deck in increasingly cold, blustery weather wore Captain Patten down. He became very ill and had to be put to bed.

When the villainous first mate demanded that he be freed to take command of the ship, Mary Patten refused, knowing that her husband distrusted him. She called the crew together and told them she would get them around the Horn and to San Francisco if they followed her commands as they did her husband's. The first mate tried to stir up a mutiny, but the crew sided with Mrs. Patten.

Neptune's Car, with Mary Patten acting as captain, slowly fought the winter gales. In a remarkable display of both courage and endurance, the young woman clung to her post and sailed the battered clipper around the Horn. While continuing up the West coast of South America, Captain Patten recovered somewhat and promptly made an error in judgment—he released the first mate and let him resume watches. The mate also soon made an error. In his effort to delay the clipper, he headed for Valparaiso. But this desperate effort to ruin the chances of *Neptune's Car* to make a good showing in the race was recognized quickly, and the traitorous mate was imprisoned again. Ordering the crew to put up all the canvas the clipper could carry, Mary Patten drove the ship to San Francisco. She made 300 miles in one day, a great surge later undone by a long period of no wind and slack sails.

Neptune's Car did not win that clipper race, but safely came in second among the three contestants, thanks to the skill and bravery of Mary Patten. Word quickly spread of how she had taken command and gained the confidence of the crew, and of her prowess in maneuvering the ship around the Horn.

Mary Patten became famous. But her fame was less important to Mrs. Patten than two other facts—her husband was still very ill, and she was pregnant. Her baby was born in March, 1857, and her husband died three months later. Four years later, Mary Patten caught typhoid fever. In a weakened condition, she contracted tuberculosis and died. She was only 23 years old.

Her story is still told to young men and women alike, and to the thousands of people who see her name on that building in the Merchant Marine Academy.

Hannah Rebecca Burgess

When Hannah Burgess married clipper captain William Burgess in 1852, she was an unlikely candidate for a seagoing heroine. Their honeymoon was a weekend trip by ferry from Boston to Cape Cod. The bride was miserably seasick the whole time, except for a few hours on the Cape. Not surprisingly, she did not accompany her husband on his first voyage on the new clipper *Whirlwind* three months later.

A year of lonely anxiety must have outweighed her fear of seasickness, because on *Whirlwind's* next voyage, Hannah went along, never having a seasick day. She discovered that she liked shipboard life and began to learn something about sailing. She read books on navigation, studied with her captain husband and became an accomplished navigator. Further, she "learned the ropes" and became a useful member of the ship's company, even weathering the wild gales that ripped at the ship trying to get around Cape Horn. Her journal recorded that on one of the stormiest nights she would "like to have been on deck even though it meant being lashed to the rigging."

Her next sea venture with her husband was on an even larger clipper, *Challenger.* Hannah was now accepted as an expert navigator–"as good as the best captain sailing," her husband and his officers believed. She had a chance to prove herself, in tragic circumstances, when after about a year and a half, Captain Burgess became very ill and could not command the clipper. By agreement with the first mate, Hannah took over command and served as navigator as they headed for the nearest port. For almost three weeks, Mrs. Burgess took care of her husband and the ship. Captain Burgess died four days before *Challenger* reached Valparaiso, Chile, in December, 1856, with Hannah Rebecca Burgess at the helm.

Mrs. Josiah Cressy

Josiah Cressy, of Marblehead, Massachusetts, was captain of *Flying Cloud,* that marvel among clippers. He and his wife, who served as his navigator, set some remarkable records with that queen of speed. They were among the first to make use of Maury's "Charts and Sailing Directions" on *Flying Cloud's* maiden voyage in 1851. That voyage, from New York to San Francisco, set a pace for all other clipper commanders to aim for: 89 days, 21 hours, a record they themselves broke by several hours in 1854.

On the clipper's fifth voyage, returning from Canton with a cargo of tea, Mrs. Cressy saved a man's life by her quick-thinking heroism. While she was in her cabin she saw a body that seemed to sail through the air past her window. She rushed on deck, gave the alarm and threw out a life buoy. Two boats were ordered out, the clipper hove to, and after several hours' search, the almost-drowned crewman was rescued. Mrs. Cressy insisted that he be brought to her cabin, where she took care of him until he was completely recovered from his narrow escape from a briny death.

The captain's wife continued as *Flying Cloud's* navigator for several years until she and her husband retired to live in Salem, Massachusetts.

Mrs. Thomas Crapo

In 1877, Captain and Mrs. Thomas Crapo sailed across the Atlantic on their honeymoon in a 19-foot whaleboat. Obviously, she was an accomplished seafarer by the end of that voyage!

Years later, her husband paid tribute to Mrs. Crapo's shipboard bravery in a book entitled *Strange But True: Life and Adventures of Captain Crapo & Wife.*

In the book, he reported on his wife's quick and heroic response in an accident at sea when Crapo was first mate on *Kaluna,* an American brig. A breaking wave crashed onto the deck of *Kaluna,* smashing the binnacle and its light, dislodging the cabin and temporarily swamping it. Mrs. Crapo, alone in the cabin, "instead of fainting as many men would have done," did what was necessary immediately. She grabbed a lamp, made her way on deck, and standing in waist-deep water, held the lamp above the compass so that the helmsman could correct the brig's course.

Norman J. Brouwer

The
Tall
Ships
Today

Norman J. Brouwer

LIBERTAD
ARGENTINA

Her great size makes the full-rigged ship *Libertad* an impressive sight. She is 336 feet long and her rig towers 165 feet above the deck. The 2,587 ton vessel, with a draft of 23 feet and a beam of 45 feet, is owned by Argentina and is used as a training ship by that nation's navy. Built of steel, she was launched in 1959, and made her first voyage to Europe in 1963.

In 1966, and again in 1976, *Libertad* won medals for the distance she traveled in 24-hour runs, while trainees made up more than half her crew. In 1966, she sailed for 2,058 miles across the Atlantic from Canada to the Irish Sea in 8½ days.

Under full sail, *Libertad* flies five jibs on her long bowsprit.

Norman J. Brouwer

ZENOBE GRAMME
BELGIUM

Belgium's contribution to the world of Tall Ships is a 92-foot ketch. This 149-ton vessel was commissioned in 1962. She has a beam of 22 feet, five inches and a draft of seven feet. Her mainmast is 95 feet tall; her 200 horsepower Diesel drives her at 10 knots. The ketch was designed for scientific research and carries a crew of 14.

ORIOLE
CANADA

Canada uses the 102-foot long steel ketch *Oriole* for sail-training for junior officers of her Navy and Naval Reserve. The ketch was built in 1921 in Boston for a Toronto yachtsman. In 1948, she was taken over by the Royal Canadian Navy and is the only commissioned yacht in that Navy.

Oriole generally cruises around Vancouver Island, but also takes part in Pacific Ocean races, including Tall Ships events. The 78-ton yacht has a beam of 19 feet, a draft of 9.6 feet and her mainmast is 94 feet high.

OUR SVANEN
CANADA

This barkentine gets her rugged appearance from her Scandinavian ancestry. She was built in Denmark, in 1922, as a Baltic trader. In 1969, *Our Svanen* was purchased by Margaret and Douglas Havers, who have rebuilt her over the years and have used her for sail-training in many places. From 1981 to 1984, she was chartered to the Royal Canadian Sea Cadet-Training Division. Her owners provide instruction, aided by crew members, some of whom are former trainees.

Svanen (which means Swan) normally carries a crew of seven and 16 trainees. With her three-masted rig, she is glorious under full, billowing sail.

The beam of this barkentine measures 22 feet, 10 inches; she has a draft of nine feet, six inches. The 119-ton ship has a rig height of 80 feet, 4,500 square feet of sail area, and is powered by a 155 horsepower Diesel. *Our Svanen* takes part in Tall Ships races.

PATHFINDER and PLAYFAIR
CANADA

The two brigantines *Pathfinder* and *Playfair* are almost identical twins. *Pathfinder*, built in 1964 at Kingston, Ontario, displaces 39 tons. Her sister, built ten years later, displaces 45 tons. They share other dimensions. Each of the two has a sparred length of 72 feet, with a waterline length of 45 feet. The beam is 15 feet, six inches, and the draft seven feet, six inches. Both steel-hulled vessels were designed by Francis MacLachlan. Each is powered by a 100 horsepower Diesel, with 15 sails totalling, 4,400 square feet.

The twin sisters sail out of Toronto on the Great Lakes and the St. Lawrence River, each carrying 18 teenaged youngsters on 12-day cruises for sail training during the summer. Many of the trainees take part in maintenance operations during the cold months. The program is run by Toronto Brigantines, Inc.

SPIRIT OF CHEMAINUS
CANADA

Among the newest of sail training vessels is the 40-ton *Spirit of Chemainus*, launched in 1985. Her hull design is based on lines taken from a Goucester sloop by Howard I. Chapelle, naval historian. At 92 feet, the new vessel is a little longer than the original. Like *Cadboro*, the first such rig to enter Victoria Harbor in 1837, *Spirit of Chemainus* is rigged as a brigantine.

The ship is owned by the Sail and Life Training Society of Victoria, British Columbia. The society explains that with this vintage sailing vessel it "aims not only to recapture the beauty of line and form represented by the last days of sail, but also to instill in her young crew the qualities of teamwork, discipline, seamanship and a sense of balance and wonder in nature."

Spirit of Chemainus was named for the small seaside town of Chemainus, which in recent years has been transformed from a quiet mill town to an art center noted for the murals painted on the exterior walls of buildings. The ship's hull is yellow cedar and fir planking on oak ribs. Her decks are fir, while the bulwarks and transom are made of mahogany and gum. Yellow and red cedar are used for the interior, which has berths for 20 trainees and four crew members.

The new brigantine has a beam of 18 feet, a draft of nine feet, six inches, and her rig is 77 feet high. Her length on deck is 65 feet. *Spirit* was build in a shed on the town's waterfront. Much of the timber was contributed by the town, which owns a forest.

Robertson II Sail and Line Training Society

ROBERTSON II
CANADA

An original Grand Banks fishing schooner, *Robertson II,* has a beam of 22 feet and a draft of 12 feet. She is a 98-ton wooden vessel, built in 1940 at Shelburne, Nova Scotia. (This is the same seacoast town where Donald McKay, famous designer and builder of clipper ships, was born.) *Robertson II* has 5,637 square feet of sail area and has a Diesel for auxiliary power. She is 130 feet long and her rig height is 109 feet.

Robertson II operates during the warm months as a sail-training vessel, taking 30 students on 10-day voyages for experience in shipboard life. She is worked by a crew of three.

This schooner is owned by the *Robertson II* Sail and Life Training Society of Victoria, British Columbia, which also owns *Spirit of Chemainus.*

Malcolm Mackenzie

ESMERALDA
CHILE

With her overall length of 353 feet the four-masted barkentine, *Esmeralda*, is the largest sailing vessel in the Western Hemisphere, edging out *Libertad* for that honor, but bowing to *Kruzenstern* for the world title. *Esmeralda* is one of the most thrilling ships to see with her voluminous array of sails flying. She was built in 1952 at Cadiz, Spain, as a sister ship to that country's *Juan Sebastian de Elcano*, from which she differs only in rigging. Her original name was *Don Juan de Austria*, but before she was completely finished, she was destroyed by fire and sold in 1953 to Chile, where she was rebuilt and re-christened.

This barkentine is a huge, steel-hulled sailing ship, carrying 332 officers, crew and cadets. *Esmeralda* usually spends half of every year on training cruises for graduates of the Chilean Naval Academy. At her bow is a Condor, Chile's national bird, holding the nation's coat-of-arms in its claws. *Esmeralda's* beam is 44 feet, her draft 23 feet. Her mast height is 165 feet.

Fast under sail or power, she can attain up to 12 knots with her 1,400 horsepower Diesel. She has a range of 8,000 miles under power at her cruising speed of eight knots.

Unlike many sail-training vessels, *Esmeralda* is armed. She carries four 5.7 centimeter guns. The ship was named for a Chilean warship credited with sea victories in the 1879 Nitrate War against Bolivia and Peru.

Malcolm Mackenzie

GLORIA
COLUMBIA

This lovely bark could well be called Colombia's gem of the ocean. She was built of steel in Bilbao, Spain, in 1968. *Gloria* is somewhat similar to *Eagle*, although 40 feet shorter, with her overall length of 255 feet. Her beam measures 35 feet and she carries 150 persons, including 15 officers, 45 crew members and 90 trainees of the Colombian Navy. She is equipped to carry provisions for remaining at sea as long as 60 days.

A winged figurehead graces the bow of the *Gloria*. With her 500 horsepower Diesel engine she is able to make 10.5 knots. Her sail area is about 15,000 square feet and her mast height is 130 feet.

One of this bark's distinguishing features is a raised bridge and enclosed pilothouse forward of the mizzenmast.

Norman J. Brouwer

DANMARK
DENMARK

No nation has a longer record in sail-training than Denmark; that country has used sail-training for at least 300 years. Today, the Danish government gives training under sail to boys, 15 to 20 years old, ambitious for careers as officers in the Danish Merchant Marine. The young men are sent for cruises on *Danmark*, a 252-foot full-rigged ship, which carries 80 trainees.

The cruises normally take six months and usually go around the world. The ship and its crew are famous for the salute they give in port, by "manning the yards." The white-uniformed crew stands on the yards, high above the deck, hands stretched out to each other.

At sea, the trainees are given intensive education in mathematics, physics, mechanical engineering and hygiene, as well as navigation, radio technique, winds and currents, meteorology and ship construction. In addition, they get the usual sail-training, performing tasks aboard ship from washing dishes to assisting the surgeon. The ship makes a point of entering and leaving ports under sail if possible.

Danmark was launched in 1932. In 1940, she happened to be in Florida when the German Army occupied Denmark. After Pearl Harbor, the ship was offered to the U.S. government, and was used as a Coast Guard training vessel, with the Danish officers in charge of instruction. In 1945, the vessel returned to her own country; in 1959, the ship was renovated and modernized.

Danmark was designed by Aage Larsen. Her hull is steel. She has a beam of 33 feet and a draft of 17 feet. The vessel carries 26 sails with a total area of 17,600 square feet and her rig is 130 feet high. With her 486 horsepower Diesel, she makes 9.5 knots in calm seas. The ship has a double bottom.

Norman J. Brouwer

GUAYAS
ECUADOR

Guayas, built in Spain in 1977 for Ecuador, is a bark very similar to Colombia's ship, *Gloria*, built in Spain a year later. Both are among the newer sail-training vessels. *Guayas*, who gets her name from the first steamship built in South America, has sailed around the world.

The 914-ton ship accommodates 180 persons. In addition to student midshipmen, she sometimes takes along honor cadets from other service academies of Ecuador.

The beam of this training ship measures 35 feet and her draft is 14 feet; she is powered by a 700 horsepower Diesel engine. Her sparred length is 268 feet; the height of her rig is 127 feet.

SIR WINSTON CHURCHILL
ENGLAND

A three-masted schooner, *Sir Winston Churchill* is a 150 foot long British sail-training vessel built in Yorkshire and launched in 1965. The ship has a beam of 27 feet, a draft of 16, and she displaces 299 tons. Sails on two of her masts are gaff-rigged, but the one on the mizzen is Marconi-rigged. She carries two square sails on her foremast; all her masts are aluminum. Her mainmast is 100 feet high. Total sail area is 8,790 feet. The training ship has a 240 horsepower auxiliary engine.

Sir Winston is operated by a crew of eight officers and three seamen and accommodates 44 cadets, 16 to 21 years of age, who are given sail-training in the British maritime tradition.

Norman J. Brouwer

BELEM
FRANCE

Belem, a 572-ton bark built in 1896, is the last survivor of France's fleet of commercial sailing vessels. She has been rescued, repatriated and restored through a great public and private effort in France after a career that ranged from lowly work hauling coal and live mules to aristocratic service as a private yacht.

Belem was built at Nantes and was first put to work transporting cocoa beans and other goods between Brazil and France. In 1914, she made a quantum leap up the social ladder when the Duke of Westminster bought her and transformed her into a sumptuous yacht accommodating 40 persons. He installed her first engines and generator, painted gun ports on her topsides to give her the appearance of an oldtime corvette, and introduced yachty-looking teak in a handrail for the dining saloon. In 1921, *Belem* was bought by another well-heeled yachtsman, A.E. Guinness, the Irish brewer, who renamed her *Fantome II*. She sailed around the world in 18 months. Next the ship passed to Italian ownership. Her name was changed to *Giorgia Cini* and her rig was changed to barkentine by the substitution of fore-and-aft sails for the square sails on her mainmast. She became a school ship for young sailors in the Adriatic from 1952 to 1976. Toward the end of that period she was sent to a shipyard in Venice for repairs.

Meanwhile interest was developing in France to regain possession of the historic ship. The National Union of Savings Banks of France came to the rescue. In 1979 a deal was made to buy the ship and tow her back to France. The following year a foundation was created to restore and preserve her. The bark rig and the original name were restored and extensive rehabilitation was planned.

Belem made a triumphant return to Paris, where she was outfitted as a museum ship. Tied up at a quay along the left bank of the Seine near the Eiffel Tower, the venerable ship and the tower joined in attracting tourists. Admission fees helped defray the cost of the extensive work needed to return *Belem* fully to sailing condition.

The ship is 180 feet in sparred length, 26.8 feet wide and has a draft of 15 feet. She is privately owned by the Fondation Belem in Paris.

Norman J. Brouwer

PALINURO
ITALY

The 227-foot barkentine, *Palinuro,* now in the Italian Navy, was formerly the *Commandant Louis Richard,* owned by France. She was built in that country, at Nantes, in 1934. Italy purchased her in 1950, renovated and renamed her.

She carries four square sails on her foremast, which is one foot taller than the mainmast. The main and mizzenmasts are gaff-rigged, with topsails. Three staysails are flown between the main and foremasts. *Palinuro* sails at speeds up to 10 knots.

The ship has a beam of 33 feet, draws 16 feet, and her rig is 115 feet high. She displaces 1,341 tons. The sail area is 9,662 feet. Her auxiliary engine is of 375 horsepower. *Palinuro* is used for specialized sail-training, including the training of harbormasters. She carries five officers, 26 seamen and 54 cadets.

Donald Callender, Jr.

AMERIGO VESPUCCI
ITALY

One of the largest of the full-rigged ships used by the navies of the world for sail-training, the 330-foot *Amerigo Vespucci* was named for the Italian navigator and explorer who lived from 1451 to 1512, and for whom America was named. The ship was built of steel in 1930, in Italy. Her beam is 50 feet, 10 inches. She carries 7 officers, a crew of 30 and 100 trainees. Her rig is 160 feet high.

Amerigo Vespucci has sailed across the Atlantic many times. One short but notable passage was in 1960, when she carried the Olympic flame from Athens to Italy. About 20 years later, she made an educational tour to countries bordering the Mediterranean, promoting control of pollution of the sea.

This ship is recognized easily not only because of her monumental size, but because she resembles a 19th Century frigate. She has rather high topsides with two bands of white at the levels of her ports on an otherwise black hull.

CORSARO II
ITALY

Corsaro II is a 50-ton schooner, 63 feet long, used for sail training of young midshipmen after graduation from the Italian Naval Academy. The vessel carries 12 officers and two petty officers. They frequently enter her in races in the North Atlantic and in the Mediterranean. The ship was built in Italy in 1960. Her beam measures 15 feet, and her main mast is 75 feet high.

Donald Callender, Jr.

NIPPON MARU
JAPAN

The four-masted bark *Nippon Maru*, 318 feet long, was built in 1930, along with her sister ship *Kaiwo Maru*. A distinctive feature of her appearance is a smokestack between her main and mizzenmasts (which are the second and third masts, aft of the foremast and forward of the rigger). Her mainmast is 145 feet high.

Nippon has crossed the Pacific several times and has appeared in New York harbor. She was renovated extensively in 1975.

This bark and her sister ship are both used to train officers for the merchant marine of Japan. They are operated by 27 officers and a crew of 48, and each trains 120 cadets at a time.

CUAUHTEMOC
MEXICO

This beautiful bark, named in honor of the last Aztec emperor of Mexico, is one of the newest Tall Ships in the world, having started her career in 1982. The Mexican Navy has had a succession of sail-training vessels and this slender, steel-hulled, square-rigged ship is the current one. She was built in Spain and is similar to the sail-training ships of Colombia, Ecuador and Paraguay. At 296 feet she is about the same size as *Eagle*.

Cuahtemoc, (pronounced "Kwow-tay-mock"), displaces 1,755.5 tons. Her beam measures 39.4 feet, her draft is 16.7 feet and her rig height is 140 feet. Owned by the Mexican Naval Academy, she sails out of Vera Cruz, carrying 90 naval cadets and 172 crew members.

Malcolm Mackenzie

CHRISTIAN RADICH
NORWAY

Any of the big school ships would make stunning appearances in a movie, but none better than the Norwegian *Christian Radich* which appeared in the film "Windjammer" in 1958.

The 205-foot *Radich* is one of the few ships with male names and there is good reason for it. The estate of Captain Christian Radich, who had been a wealthy merchant and ship owner, contributed to the commissioning of the *Radich* in 1937. The 575-ton, full-rigged ship has a steel hull. Her beam is 33 feet and her draft 15 feet. Her sails have a total area of 14,525 square feet and her rig is 128 feet high. The ship is equipped with a 600 horsepower Diesel engine that will move her at eight knots.

Radich is either a particularly fast ship among square riggers on the seas today, or is sailed with extraordinary skill, for she has won more than her share of sail-training races since 1956, when she won the Dartmouth to Lisbon race in Europe. This ship has crossed the Atlantic many times and has gone up the St. Lawrence Seaway and through the Great Lakes to Chicago, where she was a sensational attraction. It was estimated that more than 35,000 people visited *Radich* there in three days.

As many as 90 boys, 15 to 19 years of age, are given training at one time aboard *Radich*. For three months, they receive both theoretical and practical instruction in all aspects of life aboard a sailing vessel, starting with washing their own clothing and cleaning all parts of the ship. There is emphasis on safety, with instruction in fire protection, handling life boats, swimming and life-saving. When the ship is cruising, the trainees are assigned to sea duty.

As the first stage in the training of young would-be Norwegian seamen, that three months aboard the *Radich* is necessarily a strongly disciplined, rigidly structured, collective regimen. By the time the students go ashore at the end of this introductory training cruise, they will know whether a seaman's life is for them. If a young man is still enthusiastic about a career at sea after the rigors of shipboard living he receives double credit for his initial training aboard the *Radich*. If a trainee decides that the sea life is not for him, he has still benefited from an experience he will remember the rest of his life.

SØRLANDET
NORWAY

The 216-foot full-rigged ship Sørlandet is named for the southern coastal area of Norway, where she was built at the port of Kristiansand in 1927. She has been a sail-training vessel for most of her long and useful life, except during World War II.

In that period, she became an overcrowded floating prison for deserters from the German army. Some of the prisoners scuttled the ship, probably by opening sea cocks, and she sank in her harbor in northern Norway. After the war, the ship was retrieved from the frigid fiord, was renovated and returned to the mission of giving sail-training to future merchant seamen in 1948.

Years later, she was presented as a gift to the city of Kristiansand. She was repaired again, put into excellent condition to resume carrying trainees in 1980. That year, about 300 youngsters from 10 nations took part in international friendship cruises aboard Sørlandet. In 1981, the ship crossed the Atlantic four times.

Like another Norwegian sail training vessel, Christian Radich, Sørlandet has been a film star. She was in the BBC film, "All I Ask Is a Tall Ship." In addition, she has appeared in television commercials.

Sørlandet is currently owned by a foundation whose board chairman is the mayor of Kristiansand. The governments of Norway and the city pay for routine maintenance of the ship, but she relies on donations, charters and other private sources for operating income. Her owner is the Full-rigged Ship Sørlandet Non-Profit Foundation.

The 559-ton vessel's hull, masts and yards are steel. Her decks are planked with pine. She carries five levels of square sails on each of her three masts—main, lower and upper topsails, gallant and royal. In addition to those 15 square sails, there are 13 fore-and-aft sails: five jibs, a spanker and storm spanker, three mizzen staysails and three main staysails. Most of the sails are of polyester fabric, and their area is 10,360 square feet.

Sørlandet accommodates 70 trainees and 19 crew members. She has tanks for 40 tons of fresh water and has a desalination plant capable of producing three tons of fresh water a day. A 564-horsepower Diesel powers the ship; electricity is produced by a six-cylinder generator. She makes eight knots under power.

The ship carries 400 tons of stone ballast. Her beam is 29.1 feet and her draft is 14.5 feet. Her overall length, excluding the 20-foot bowsprit, is 186 feet. The mainmast is 115 feet above the waterline.

ZAWISZA CZARNY II
POLAND

Zawisza Czarny II is a 141-foot, three-masted schooner but unlike the standard schooner, her mainmast is the foremast and her other masts decrease in height toward the stern. Her tallest mast measures 93 feet. She is gaff-rigged, with topsails, and carries 5,918 square feet of sail. The vessel was built in 1952 at Gdansk. Her beam is 22 feet, her draft 14 feet and she has a 300 horsepower engine. Displacement is 197 tons.

This schooner is used for sail-training for officers of the Polish merchant marine. The Polish Navy also uses sail-training vessels.

Malcolm Mackenzie

SAGRES II
PORTUGAL

This bark from Portugal is a dazzling sight, as is her elder sister-ship, the United States *Eagle*. Both are 295 feet long. *Sagres II* has an unforgettable appearance, because she wears the Maltese Cross on her square sails, and sports a bust of Prince Henry the Navigator for her figurehead. Her tallest mast is 142 feet aloft.

Sagres II was built in 1938 in Germany and, with *Eagle,* became the property of the United States at the end of the World War II. Brazil became her owner in 1948 and Portugal bought her in 1962 to replace *Sagres I.*

The current *Sagres* normally carries 243 persons aboard: 10 officers, a crew of 153 and 80 cadets. Her speed under power is nine knots, and she has a 40 foot beam.

The ship's name comes from the promontory near Cape St. Vincent in southwestern Portugal, from which many explorers departed in the 15th Century. Prince Henry, who was more of a sponsor than a navigator himself, died there in 1460. Shipwatchers admiring the figurehead should honor Prince Henry as one of the earliest backers of oceanic exploration, (from Portugal to the west coast of Africa).

The spanker—the fore-and-aft sail on the bark's third and smallest mast—is in three sections, divided by two gaffs. Many spankers are in two parts, separated by a single gaff.

Sagres II has a sail area of about 20,000 square feet. She carries 52 tons of oil for her two Diesel engines of 750 horsepower each, which give her a top speed of 9.4 knots and a range of 5,450 miles at her cruising speed of 7.5 knots. Earlier in her career, this ship was named *Guanabara* when owned by Brazil, and *Albert Leo Schlageter* when owned by Germany.

Norman J. Brouwer

MIRCEA
RUMANIA

The 270 foot long sail-training bark *Mircea* is a near twin of the Soviet *Tovarisch*, and was built in 1938 for Rumania, at the Blohm & Voss shipyard at Hamburg, Germany, where a series of square-riggers was built in the 1930's. She has a large smokestack between her main and mizzenmasts, like the *Nippon Maru's*. The steel-hulled vessel has a beam of 39 feet and a draft of 17 feet. Her highest mast is 135 feet, her sail area is more than 18,000 square feet and she is powered by a 1,100 horsepower Diesel. She displaces 1,760 tons.

Mircea was named for a Rumanian prince who was a war hero of the 14th Century. A figurehead representing the prince, with his crown and mustache, is at the bow.

The ship is sailed by 40 officers and 50 crew members, and has room for 120 trainees.

Norman J. Brouwer

KRUZENSTERN
SOVIET UNION

The largest of all the sail-training vessels, larger even than *Esmeralda* and her sister ship, *Juan Sebastian de Elcano,* is another four-masted vessel, the Soviet Union's 378-foot bark, *Kruzenstern.* Unlike most other national sail-training ships, she is attached to the Ministry of Fisheries, rather than to the Navy or the Coast Guard.

This mammoth ship accommodates 236 persons, including 26 officers, 50 crew members and 160 trainees. Her beam is a broad 46 feet, her draft is 25 feet, and her sail area is more than 36,000 voluminous square feet. Her mainmast is 162 feet high.

This vessel was named for Ivan F. Kruzenstern who, in 1803 to 1806, led the first Russian round-the-world scientific expedition, and subsequently published several works based on that long voyage.

Kruzenstern is distinguished not only by her heroic size, but by her lifeboats, which are carried high above the deck in davits. She has a double spanker and topsail on her fourth mast.

The ship, built in 1926, hauled nitrate from Chile, and grain from Australia, before she was taken over by the Soviet Union, in 1946. Previously, she had been named *Padua.*

Norman J. Brouwer

TOVARISCH
SOVIET UNION

The Soviet Union's bark, *Tovarisch,* is one of four similar but not identical ships built in Hamburg, Germany. The others are *Eagle, Mircea,* and *Sagres II. Tovarisch* was built in 1933 and was originally the *Gorch Fock* of the German Navy, which has another ship by that name now.

Tovarisch has a beam of 39 feet, four inches and her draft is 17 feet. She carries 18,400 square feet of sails. Her mainmast is 135 feet and her sparred length is 270 feet.

The vessel sank in 1945 and was refloated by Soviet salvage workers three years later. In 1951, she joined the Soviet Navy as a sail-training vessel. (The Soviet Union had a previous ship by the same name—a four-masted bark that had once been called *Lauriston.*)

There are several acceptable ways of spelling *Tovarisch,* which is, of course, an English rendition of the Russian. Some prefer to spell it "Tovaristsch". However it's spelled, the word means comrade.

Norman J. Brouwer

JUAN SEBASTIAN DE ELCANO
SPAIN

Here is a huge sailing vessel—one of the world's largest—rigged as a topsail schooner. She is a marvelous sight to behold, resembling an out-sized version of recreational yachts, 352 feet long.

Far from being an overgrown wind and water-borne plaything, Spain's *Juan Sebastian De Elcano* is an impressive sail-training ship and one of the few four-masted sailing ships afloat. Her draft is 22.7 feet and her beam is 44 feet. (In spite of the masculine name, this ship, like all others, requires the feminine gender.) She carries 407 persons: 24 officers, a crew of 173 and 210 trainees.

Juan Sebastian is unmistakably an ocean sailer. At 164 feet, her mainmast is too high for many large bridges.

She is a sister ship to Chile's *Esmeralda.* The two have the same hulls but different rigging. While the Spanish ship is a topsail schooner, the Chilean version is a four-masted barkentine. The Spanish ship carries two saluting guns.

Juan Sebastian was named for the first circumnavigator of the world—the man who, after the death of Magellan, succeeded to the command of the 1519-1523 expedition.

The Granger Collection

GORCH FOCK
WEST GERMANY

The 295-foot steel bark *Gorch Fock,* named for a writer of sea stories who died in 1916, is West Germany's sail-training vessel. She takes 200 trainees at a time, in addition to her 46 officers and 21 crew members. She was built at Hamburg in 1958 by the Blohm & Voss shipyard, which has built many large sail training ships.

Gorch Fock's 22 sails add up to more than 21,000 square feet of sail area. At her bow is a golden eagle figurehead; the rest of her hull is white. The ship has been making two training cruises each year. In one, she goes through the Baltic Sea to the North Sea. In a longer cruise, she ventures to the West Indies or to the East coast of the United States.

The ship's rig is 140 feet high, her beam is 39 feet four inches, and her draft is 16 feet five inches. Her Diesel generates 800 horsepower.

JADRAN
YUGOSLAVIA

Yugoslavia's 190-foot topsail schooner, *Jadran,* is one of the larger schooners devoted to sail-training. She displaces 720 tons, has a beam of 29 feet two inches and a draft of 13 feet eight inches. *Jadran* was built at Hamburg in 1932 and served in the Italian Navy as *Marco Polo* during World War II.

This ship has 8,600 square feet of sails and a 375 horsepower engine which will move *Jadran* at eight knots. She accommodates 150 cadets.

SEA CLOUD
WEST GERMANY

The largest and most luxurious privately-owned square-rigger in the world is *Sea Cloud,* a four-masted bark. With a sparred length of 316 feet, she is longer than the U.S. Coast Guard's *Eagle*.

Sea Cloud was built in 1931 in Germany as an elegant yacht for Marjorie Merriweather Post, heiress to a cereal fortune, and her husband, Edward F. Hutton. The steel-hulled vessel cost $1.2 million in 1931 dollars. During World War II, the U.S. Navy leased the ship for convoy duty.

After the war, Mrs. Post retained her palatial yacht for four years, and she is reported to have spent $3 million in refitting and operating costs.

Sea Cloud's next owner was General Rafael Trujillo, dictator of the Dominican Republic, who renamed the ship *Patria*. A later owner changed her name to *Atarna* and used the ship as a floating university.

The name has reverted to the original *Sea Cloud*. She was again refurbished in 1978, and partially rebuilt inside to have more staterooms, which currently number 41. Now, she is an opulent cruise ship plying the Caribbean and Mediterranean with private parties.

Sea Cloud's dimensions are impressive: The ship displaces 2,323 tons. She is 49 feet wide and has a draft of 16.5 feet. She has four 9-cylinder Diesel engines driving two propellers. Those engines have an output of 6,000 horsepower and can move the ship at 15 knots. Her range is 10,000 miles and her crew numbers 60.

The 49-foot beam allows ample room for a sumptuous main saloon with deck to ceiling bookcases and a grand piano. The dining saloon is also capacious. The ship has her own small "hospital" on one of the three decks.

The ship's sail plan shows four jibs and staysails at the bowsprit and bow, three masts with five square sails each and the jigger mast at the stern with a spanker. Above the spanker is a topsail called in this case a jigger upper staysail. In addition, when the wind is right, the ship can spread six staysails between the masts. There is no doubt that *Sea Cloud* can spread a glorious cloud of canvas.

Norman J. Brouwer

ALEXANDRIA
UNITED STATES

The three-masted topsail schooner *Alexandria* is a familiar sight at gatherings of Tall Ships and waterfront celebrations, distinguished by her red sails, including two square sails at the top of her foremast. She was widely known under her former name of Lindø, which was changed in 1983 when she was acquired by the Alexandria Seaport Foundation.

The ship has had a varied history, with different rigs, different missions and different engines since she was launched in 1929 in Sweden as *Yngve,* and put to work as a bulk cargo carrier in the Baltic and North Seas. After 10 years of service, which included fishing for herring north of Iceland, she was sold and renamed *Lindö,* a Swedish term standing for "island of Linden trees." In 1957 she was re-rigged as a two-masted vessel, and 10 years later she was altered again to become a motor ship.

Major changes were made in 1975 when the ship was rebuilt in Denmark, converted for passenger carrying and re-rigged as a topsail schooner. The Danish punctuation of the name was used, making it *Lindø.* An 185-horsepower Diesel was installed, replacing a 150 horsepower engine which had followed the original 90 horsepower plant. The vessel then was used in the charter trade in the Caribbean and began taking part in Tall Ships races. In 1976 she placed third in her class in the race from England to New York. She took second place in her class in 1980 in a race from Boston to Norway. In 1982 she appeared in the film "The Island," and the following year she arrived in Alexandria and was re-named for the city. There she promotes interest in the city's historic seaport and in the foundation's education programs in celestial navigation and wooden boat building. In addition, teenagers get apprentice sail training on the ship.

Alexandria has an overall length of 125 feet. The vessel displaces 176 tons, and has a beam of 22 feet and a draft of 10. Heavily constructed, her planking is three-inch oak and her frames are eight-inch oak. Her 11 sails offer more than 7,000 square feet of area to the wind. The ship is luxurious below decks, where she has a spacious salon and five double staterooms.

ADVENTURESS
UNITED STATES

The 101-foot wooden schooner *Adventuress* has had a varied history since she was built by the Rice Brothers at East Boothbay, Maine, in 1913 as a yacht. She was first used to collect Arctic specimens in the Bering Sea for a museum, and then moved to the West Coast to be used by San Francisco Bay pilots. After changing hands several more times she was acquired in the early 1960's by Youth Adventure, Inc., a non-profit organization offering sail-training for young people.

Sailing out of Seattle, Washington, *Adventuress* takes 25 to 30 trainees at a time, usually for eight-day sessions in the summer and for weekends the rest of the year. The vessel sails mainly in Puget Sound. In addition to learning seamanship and shipboard duties, the trainee may be given instruction in marine biology or other subjects.

Adventuress has a beam of 21 feet, a draft of 12, and displaces 82 tons. Her sail area is 4,5000 square feet, and she carries a 250 horsepower Diesel.

BOWDOIN
UNITED STATES

The heavily built 88-foot wooden schooner *Bowdoin* has an illustrious history in Arctic exploration and an ardent following among those who went with her and Admiral Donald B. MacMillan on 26 voyages to the far north. The crew members were not seasoned sailors; they were students and research scientists who paid their way.

Bowdoin was built in 1921. More than 50 years later, when the ship was deteriorating, many of those early crew members organized a rescue effort. Between 1980 and 1986, the vessel was thoroughly restored, made ready for certification under the School Vessels Act, and prepared to enter a new phase in her long history as a floating educational and research institution.

Bowdoin, named after MacMillan's alma mater, was designed by William Hand to specifications based on MacMillan's experience in being marooned in the Arctic for four years, for lack of a rescue ship strong enough to penetrate the ice. *Bowdoin* is phenomenally strong. She is double-planked and double-framed with white oak and sheathed in a five-foot wide belt of inch-and-a-half ironwood. For even greater toughness, she has an 1,800-pound steel nose, and a bow designed to rise over ice and crush it if she cannot push through it. Her original engine could operate on a mixture of kerosene, whale oil and seal oil, if required.

The ship's career as an education and research enterprise started in 1921, when she carried an expedition to Greenland for work in mapping, zoology, botany, meteorology and terrestrial magnetism. She has 300,000 miles of Arctic voyages of exploration to her credit. During World War II, *Bowdoin* served as a pilot vessel for other ships entering and leaving the west coast of Greenland. In 1980, she was listed on the National Register of Historic Places.

In 1959, when MacMillan was 84, he gave *Bowdoin* to a museum, but she was not maintained. In 1967, MacMillan organized an association to get the ship back and rescue her from decaying. She was partially restored and was able to make a sentimental journey to Provincetown Harbor, Massachusetts, where MacMillan, then in his 90's saw her for the last time.

After several other ups and downs in charter work and in sail-training, in 1980, *Bowdoin* was taken to the old Percy & Small Shipyard at the Maine Maritime Museum in Bath, to be rebuilt by apprentices and expert shipwrights, including John Nugent, who had worked on the ship for many years, and had served for a time as her skipper. Five watertight bulkheads were installed, among other improvements.

Fully restored, *Bowdoin* has returned to educational work with a program with the Boston public schools. Pupils explore the waters near Boston aboard the ship during the school year. In the summer, *Bowdoin* engages in other sail training.

Bowdoin was designed to be similar to Gloucester fishing schooners. She displaces 66 tons, and has a beam of 21 feet and draft of 9.5 feet. Her baldheaded gaff-rigged mainsail and foresail and her staysail and flying jib add up to 2,900 square feet of sails. One of her special features is an "ice barrel"—an Arctic crow's nest, mounted on the starboard spreader of her foremast. She has a 100-horsepower Diesel. She is owned proudly by the Schooner Bowdoin Association at Rockland, Maine.

CLIPPER CITY
UNITED STATES

Clipper City was built in 1984-85 in Green Cove Springs, Florida, as a steel-hulled likeness of a clipper built in 1854 in Wisconsin. She is a 158-foot topsail schooner, carrying two square sails on the upper part of her foremast. The vessel has a beam of 27.5 feet, and a draft of 5.5 feet with centerboard up, and 14 feet with the board lowered. Her sail area is 8,200 square feet. Masts are steel; decks are yellow pine. Her rig is 135 feet high.

The ship was built to offer public excursions and is based at the Inner Harbor of Baltimore, Maryland. She can carry up to 149 passengers. Food and beverages are available during her three-hour trips.

While *Clipper City* has the outward appearance of a sailing vessel of the 19th Century, she is a very modern ship down below. Her galley is all electric, she has air-conditioning and heating equipment, whirlpools in two private baths connected to two of her staterooms, and modern decor in her salon.

ELISSA
UNITED STATES

The iron bark *Elissa,* built in 1877, has been rescued from a rusty grave and restored to a position of honor and respect in Galveston, Texas. The only restored square-rigger in the southwestern United States is a handsome ship with a sparred length of 202 feet. She was built at the Alexander Hall shipyard in Aberdeen, Scotland, as a cargo vessel—although a small one for that period.

Early in her history, *Elissa* called at Galveston, in 1883 and again in 1886, at a time when that city handled more cotton than any other port in the world, and when a score of sailing vessels would be at anchor in Galveston harbor any day.

In her long life, *Elissa* had owners in Finland, England, Norway and Greece, and several names, among them *Fjeld, Gustav* and *Christophoros.* Her rig was also modified a few times. About 1959, while under Greek ownership, she lost her sailing ship bow in a collision, and became a motor cargo ship. In 1966 she was being used for smuggling untaxed cigarettes between Yugoslavia and Italy, but soon she was considered worn out and too expensive to repair. She was rusting away in a remote corner of the Piraeus harbor when she was found by a marine archaeologist.

The Galveston Historical Foundation bought the ship in 1975 and started the long and expensive process of restoring her and bringing her to Texas. Partially restored, the old ship was towed to Galveston in 1979. *Elissa* was able to enter the Gulf of Mexico under full sail in 1982. Her resurrection had cost $4.5 million...and a few year's work of a large corps of volunteers.

Elissa has a beam of 28 feet and her mainmast rises 99 feet above the deck. She carries 245 tons of ballast. The ship's hull is riveted iron, partially replaced by welded steel. Her fore and mainmasts, lower yards and bowsprit are welded steel. Birdseye maple, teak and pine were used for the ship's interior.

THE SHIPS

Galveston's ship has 19 sails with a total area of 12,000 square feet. Formerly a pure sailing vessel, *Elissa* had no engine until she was prepared to sail to New York to participate in Liberty Week in 1986. Earlier when she went for her annual day sails each September she had to be towed out of the harbor before her crew of trained volunteers could take over.

When in Galveston *Elissa* is open every day for self-guided tours and is available for private gatherings. The Galveston Historical Foundation has a 20-minute film telling the story of *Elissa's* discovery and painstaking restoration as a maritime museum. The vessel has a 16-foot dinghy built for her by a graduate of the Apprenticeshop of Rockport, Maine.

Galveston Historical Foundation

EAGLE
U.S.A.

The beautiful bark, *Eagle,* is the sail-training vessel of the U.S. Coast Guard, carrying 180 trainees in addition to 19 officers and a crew of 46, for a total of 245 persons on board. She was built in Germany for sail-training in 1936 and was acquired by the United States as part of Germany's war reparations after having served as a cargo ship in World War II. The 295-foot ship is virtually unchanged under American ownership, except that the fore-and-aft sail on the mizzenmast is a single gaff spanker instead of a double. Her hull is steel; her rig is 148 feet high and her beam is 39 feet; her draft is 17 feet. *Eagle* displaces 1,784 tons.

Trainees handling *Eagle* must learn to deal with more than 25,300 square feet of

Norman J. Brouwer

sails and more than 20 miles of rigging, as well as her 700 horsepower Diesel engine. Cadets in the lower classes of the Coast Guard Academy learn to serve as the ship's crew, while the upper classmen and women serve as her officers.

There are three sister ships of *Eagle* owned by other nations: *Mircea* of Romania, *Sagres II* of Portugal and *Tovarisch II* of the Soviet Union.

Eagle goes on one to five-week cruises from her base at New London, Connecticut, during the warm months. She can sail up to 18 knots under favorable wind conditions. Under power, she can make 10.5 knots and has a range of 5,450 miles cruising at 7.5 knots.

Philadelphia Ship Presentation Guild

GAZELA OF PHILADELPHIA
UNITED STATES

The barkentine *Gazela* is remarkable because she is the oldest and largest wooden square rigger still able to sail. Her sparred length is 177 feet, 10 inches. She was formerly the Portuguese fishing vessel *Gazela Primeira* and in that role she sailed every Spring from Lisbon to the Grand Banks to launch her 30 dories from which her men fished for cod. She was built of pine in Portugal in 1883. According to Portuguese legend, the pine was planted in 1460 by Prince Henry the Navigator, specifically for shipbuilding. *Gazela* was first rigged as a topsail schooner and may have served as a whaler before 1900, when she was converted to a barkentine to become a fishing ship.

Originally, the ship relied on sail power alone. She was modernized in 1938 with the addition of a Diesel auxiliary engine along with two generators and an engine to power her windlass. However, the old hand-operated windlass is still in its place.

Visitors going below on the ship can see the extremely crowded conditions in which the fishermen slept, two to a bunk, in three tiers of bunks in the narrow forecastle.

Gazela has a draft of 16 feet, eight inches and carries 8,910 square feet of sail; her beam measures 27 feet, and her mast height is 93 feet, four inches. She is owned by the City of Philadelphia through the Penn's Landing Corporation, and she can be seen at Penn's Landing, on the Delaware River near the foot of Spruce Street.

Volunteers of the Philadelphia Ship Preservation Guild help to maintain and sail the ship.

HARVEY GAMAGE
UNITED STATES

In 1973, the Harvey Gamage shipyard in South Bristol, Maine, built this 115-foot schooner, named for the master shipbuilder. He has many other wooden vessels to his credit, including *Clearwater,* the Hudson River crusading sloop, and *Shenandoah,* a topsail schooner that sails out of Martha's Vineyard in the summer months.

Harvey Gamage has a beam of 23 feet, seven inches, a draft of nine feet, seven inches and displaces 129 tons. Her sail area is 4,200 square feet. The schooner has a Diesel engine of 120 horsepower. Her rig is 91 feet high. She sails out of Charlotte Amalie in the Virgin Islands in the winter and out of Rockland, Maine, in the summer, carrying passengers on cruises or groups of young people for sail-training.

PIONEER
UNITED STATES

Pioneer is a gaff-rigged, steel hulled schooner whose hundredth birthday was in 1985. South Street Seaport's active sailing vessel celebrated during that summer, spreading her sails and fame as she cruised to the Delaware River and Chesapeake Bay. Along the way, she docked at river and bayside ports, took local admirers for short sails, and invited curious visitors to come aboard and get to know something about this hardy old lady.

Pioneer was built in 1885 at Marcus Hook, Pennsylvania, on the Delaware River, by Pioneer Iron Works, which gave her the job of hauling sand for the foundry. She was unusual in design and construction. First, she was very beamy: her width of 22 feet is more than one-third her length on deck of 65 feet. Probably the great beam, coupled with her shallow draft, enabled her to carry a large quantity of sand to where the cargo could be loaded readily. A long jibboom gives *Pioneer* an overall length of 102 feet.

The schooner has a second unusual feature: her hull was made of wrought iron. Most ships of her period were made of wood. A third point is that *Pioneer* has a flat bottom, which contributes to her shallow draft of 4.6 feet with her oak centerboard up. Draft plunges to 16 feet with the board fully lowered.

In her long career, *Pioneer* had many owners and was put through many changes in use, in rig, in her hull and in power. She began as a sloop, became a schooner. At one time, her masts were removed and she was a cargo vessel, hauling oil. At the nadir of her working life, she was abandoned to rust away. She was rescued and restored by Russell Grinnell Jr., of Gloucester, Massachusetts, who recognized the beauty of the old sailing ship. He had the rusted wrought iron hull replated with steel, and installed the current schooner rig. After his death the museum acquired the ship, put in an 85-horsepower Perkins Diesel, and added lifelines required for carrying passengers.

At one time in her museum life, *Pioneer* was used for two-week voyages for patients from drug-rehabilitation centers, exposing them to the physical and emotional challenges of shipboard life, safely away from drugs for weeks at a time. Now she earns her keep by carrying passengers around New York Harbor on short sails, and by taking out school children who are taught something about the ship and how she is sailed, about the importance of the New York Harbor in the nation's history of shipbuilding and commerce, and as the welcoming port for millions of immigrants for hundreds of years.

Sailing on *Pioneer* is a delight. Her low freeboard—only three feet—gives one impression of being close to the water, as in a small yacht. And she has ample sail area to drive her iron hull smartly, even in light air. Of course, because of the combination of her schooner rig and flat bottom, she will not come about in less than 120 degrees, which means that, like many square-rigged ships, this handsome schooner sails well only on a reach and downwind. Her working sails are a jib, a club-footed staysail, a foresail and a generous mainsail overhanging the square stern.

South Street Seaport Museum

STEPHEN TABER
UNITED STATES

Stephen Taber was built in 1871 and is still sailing. The 115-foot gaff-rigged schooner is said to be the oldest documented sailing vessel in continuous service in the United States, and she has the distinction of being on the National Register of Historic Places. (The register, maintained by the National Park Service, is mostly of historic houses and other firmly fixed places, but includes a few ships even if their "places" happen to be movable.)

The lovely old lady is little changed from the original. She has no auxiliary engine on board; she has a yawl boat to give her a push when needed. Cooking is done on a wood stove as in the old days.

Taber has been rebuilt several times in her more than 100 years. In 1900 she was in an accident in the Narrows at the entrance to New York harbor and had to be repaired extensively. More work was done on her in 1933 and again in 1984.

Sometime in the early 1940s, *Taber* came on hard times and was out of service for two years. Providentially, she was rescued in 1945 by Captain Frederick B. Guild of Castine, Maine, who has saved several historic ships and operated them in the Maine windjammer fleet. He bought the ailing schooner and with the help of her former owner, Captain Fred Wood, restored *Taber,* getting her in top shape for her new career as a passenger carrier. She began adding zest to Maine coastal vacations in 1946, when she operated as a day-sailer. The following year with accommodations installed, she began the week-long cruises she is still providing, sailing out of Camden, Maine.

The schooner's length on deck is 68 feet, and she has a beam of 22.5 feet and a draft of five feet. She displaces 50 tons and has 3,300 square feet of sails. Her rig height is 93 feet to the tip of her flagpole. In deference to her 22 passengers, *Taber* has running water and electric lights in her cabins.

Passengers on *Taber* not only experience the delights of sailing along the Maine coast, but see first hand what can be achieved in restoring and preserving historic ships.

SPIRIT OF MASSACHUSETTS
UNITED STATES

The 138-ton *Spirit of Massachusetts,* commissioned in 1984, is a 125-foot gaff-rigged fishing schooner with topsails. She was built outdoors at the Charlestown Navy Yard at Boston, Massachusetts, by New England Historic Seaport. The ship was designed by Melbourne Smith, who built both *Pride of Baltimore* and *Californian.* The owners call her *SSS Spirit of Massachusetts,* with the letters standing for "Sailing School Ship." Her triple mission is to serve as a training ship for sea education programs, to prove herself a goodwill ambassador for the Commonwealth of Massachusetts, and to be a charter vessel for day sails, for dockside receptions and special events.

The seaport views *Spirit* as a descendant of the Edward Burgess –designed *Fredonia,* a Gloucester fishing schooner widely imitated in the fishing fleets of New England between 1890 and 1910. She may thus be regarded as a "type replica." Her hull has a V-shaped bottom and rounded topsides.

Much of the wood used in building this ship came from the eastern United States. The white oak for her frames was found in Massachusetts, while most of the longleaf pine for the hull planking and interior surfaces came from the South. Other woods used include locust, white pine, tamarack, red spruce and green heart–a tropical hardwood resistant to rot, used in the keel.

Frames for *Spirit* were assembled from four to 14 futtocks (frame sections), fastened together with trunnels (tree nails or pegs), of black locust from Pennsylvania. She was built using traditional methods and tools of the old days–the adze, and old "spuds" and "slicks", which are large chisels. These were augmented by modern power tools, including chain saws and powered planes and drills. Unlike the fishing schooners she resembles, *Spirit of Massachusetts* has the latterday advantage of outside lead ballast, bolted to her keel.

She has a beam of 24 feet and a draft of 10 feet. The white-hulled schooner's top mast truck is 100.6 feet above the waterline. She can accommodate a crew of 10. She daysails with 50 passengers and can host 75 persons at dockside. Powered by a 130 horsepower Diesel, she carries 585 gallons of fuel. She also has tanks for 600 gallons of water.

WELCOME
UNITED STATES

There are without doubt many vessels named *Welcome.* At least two are replicas, but neither is a reproduction of the square-rigged vessel of that name in which William Penn arrived in Philadelphia in 1682. One is a 60-foot wooden topsail schooner, built in 1975 at South Dartmouth, Massachusetts, modelled after a U.S. revenue cutter of about 1815. She is gaff-rigged and carries a square sail on her mast.

Another *Welcome* is a sloop with a square sail and a square topsail on her mast. This one was built as an exhibit at Fort Mackinac, and is based at Mackinaw City, Michigan. A replica of a British armed sloop of the 1770's, she sails the Great Lakes in the summer.

Her overall length is 55 feet, and she has a beam of 16 feet, and a draft of six feet. The rig height on this 65-ton vessel is 73 feet.

Marcus Halevi

Albert Cizauskas, Jr.

WESTERN UNION
UNITED STATES

Western Union, a gaff-rigged schooner, used to have a special mission and now she has another, equally interesting. She was built in 1939 in Key West, and until 1973 her job was to lay and maintain cables for the Western Union Telegraph Company. She is the last of the vessels that performed that service until satellites made underwater cables obsolete. Since 1974, she has been a specialized sail-training ship, catering to the needs of troubled youngsters in the Ocean Quest program.

The 130-foot long ship was built of long-leaf yellow pine planking over mahogany frames. Much of the hardware on *Western Union* is about 100 years old, having been "inherited" from the *John W. Atkins*, her predecessor in the cable work.

In 1977, new masts were installed in *Western Union*, and her deck was renewed with flooring from an old Maryland tobacco barn.

This schooner had a memorable adventure soon after the Bay of Pigs invasion, when she was still trying to maintain the cables in the Caribbean. While working near Cuba, *Western Union* was confronted by three gunboats that tried to force her to motor to a Cuban port. The captain pretended to have engine trouble and slowed down. Although ordered to stay off the air waves, he managed to radio the U.S. Coast Guard. Navy jets soon appeared overhead and *Western Union* came about and sailed off.

Now *Western Union*, with about 20 trainees aboard, continues to sail year round from her base at Fort Mifflin in Philadelphia. She has a beam of 23 feet, six inches and a draft of seven feet, six inches. The 91-ton ship has a rig 96 feet high, with which she carries 5,000 square feet of sails. She is powered by twin Diesels.

VICTORY CHIMES
UNITED STATES

The three-masted schooner *Victory Chimes*, said to be the largest passenger-carrying sailing vessel in the United States, has an overall length of 170 feet. She boasts 23 staterooms and carries 45 passengers plus a crew of six.

Victory Chimes, a mainstay of the Maine windjammer fleet for many years, is a schooner ram, a flat-bottomed wooden ship designed and built by J. M. C. Moore at Bethel, Delaware, between 1899 and 1911. The fourteenth of 21 rams Moore built, she was launched in 1900 as *Edwin and Maud*, named for the children of her first captain. At that time many ships were built at Bethel, on a branch of the Nanticoke River, because oak was available nearby. She is the only ram remaining of 27 built in the area.

The ship was used as a cargo hauler on Chesapeake Bay and along the East Coast before being reconditioned and outfitted for passenger service in 1954 by Capt. Frederick B. Guild of Castine, Maine. Guild helped to preserve several ships in his long career carrying passengers under sail. He owned *Victory Chimes* for 31 years. He is said to have named the ship for another that was launched on Armistice Day of World War I and was given the joyous title.

All of the ship's original ceiling planks of pine are in place, as are most of the yellow pine planks of her deck. Captain Guild added timbers to her long keel to straighten and strengthen it.

Victory Chimes has a straight-sided hull, painted green with a white top. She has a beam of 24 feet and a draft of 8.5 feet and her masts are 80 feet high. She puts up three huge gaff-headed sails without topsails, and flies two jibs and a club-footed staysail forward.

Modernized with electric lights, hot and cold running water in the staterooms and flush toilets, and equipped with radar, *Victory Chimes* does not have an engine for propulsion, although she has one for raising the anchor. She is attended by a yawl boat—a small boat with a powerful engine—to push her when needed.

In 1985 Captain Guild retired and sold the ship to Jerry Jubie, a banker, and Ted Rosenthal, a naval architect, who planned to shift her base to Duluth, Minnesota, and put her in passenger service on Lake Superior during the summer months.

Captain Kim McGowan

WHEN & IF
UNITED STATES

This wooden schooner with the tantalizing name was designed by John Alden and built in 1939, at Wiscasset, Maine, for General George Patton. One can speculate that the name implies "when and if I have the time, we'll sail together."

In fact, *When & If* was donated to the Landmark School of Pride's Crossing, Massachusetts, by a later owner than the famous general, and is now used in a summer seamanship program. All students of the Landmark School spend a week aboard *When & If*, learning about sailing and the comraderie and cooperation of shipboard life.

The schooner also participates in fund-raising events for community organizations by taking individuals for short sails. She often sails in Penobscot Bay during the summer program and takes part in Tall Ships events.

When & If has an overall length of 80 feet and is 63 feet, five inches on deck. Her beam is 15 feet one inch and her draft, eight feet eight inches. Her rig is 85 feet high and she may be indentified by her sail number: 92. The schooner has a 150 horsepower Diesel.

WESTWARD
UNITED STATES

Westward is a staysail schooner with a steel hull, built in Germany and launched in 1961. She has 7,000 square feet of sail and her mainmast is 100 feet high.

Sailing in the Atlantic off New England in the summer and in the Caribbean and the Gulf of Mexico in the winter, this 125-foot ship is busy all year as the vehicle for marine education at the college level. She carries 24 students plus faculty and crew. The students help to run the ship in addition to attending classes and doing research projects.

Westward is based in Woods Hole, Massachusetts, and is owned by the Sea Education Association.

LITTLE JENNIE
UNITED STATES

The bugeye ketch and the skipjack are the two best known traditional wooden work boats of Chesapeake Bay watermen, used mainly for dredging oysters, and both are descendants of the log canoes made by the native Americans. *Little Jennie* is a bugeye built in 1884 at Solomons, Maryland, by J. T. Marsh.

Little Jennie was put to many tasks. She was engaged in oystering early in her years on the water. Later, she became a recreational yacht and a hauler of wheat and watermelons. During the prohibition era, with engines installed and masts temporarily removed, she became a rum runner.

The old bugeye was partially restored in 1976, but then was allowed to deteriorate for seven years before she was rescued by William T. Perks, who bought her and organized a team of volunteers that undertook a full restoration. New laminated white oak frames and three watertight bulkheads were installed as part of the refurbishment of *Little Jennie.* She returned to the water in August, 1985.

Now she is owned by Operation Little Jennie, Inc., a non-profit corporation based at Centerport, New York.

YOUNG AMERICA
UNITED STATES

Young America is a rare ship for two reasons—she is a square-rigger built in America and her hull is not built of wood or steel, but of ferro-cement, a material somewhat similar to concrete, made with a thick wire mesh covered by a special form of cement.

She is a brigantine operated by the Young America Marine Education Society in Atlantic City, New Jersey. In 1985, her rigging was being rebuilt and her future mission was unclear, except that she will continue to be based at Atlantic City. In the past she has been used for sail-training.

The vessel is 130 feet long and has a rig 91 feet high.

CAPITAN MIRANDA
URUGUAY

The sail-training vessel of Uruguay's Navy is the *R.O.U. Capitan Miranda.* (The initials stand for "Republica Oriental del Uruguay.") The ship, a 205-foot, three-masted staysail schooner, was built in Spain in 1930, and started life as a survey vessel attached to the country's hydrographic office.

In 1977 she was renovated and given modern rigging and sails, demonstrating that she can reach a speed of 10.5 knots and make a day's run of 240 miles in favorable conditions.

Capitan Miranda takes 35 midshipmen at a time after their graduation from the naval academy at Montevideo. They fill the roles of both officers and seamen in all parts of the ship for four months of sail-training.

She has crossed the Atlantic several times and has sailed around Cape Horn. The ship is of wooden construction, with a beam of 27 feet and a draft of 12 feet. She displaces 441 tons and is powered by an 800 horsepower Diesel. Her rig is 130 feet high.

Malcolm Mackenzie

SIMON BOLIVAR
VENEZUELA

Venezuela's 270 foot bark is among the newest of the world's large Tall Ships. She finished her first voyage in 1981. This handsome ship was built in Spain and was named for "the great liberator" of South America, who, incidentally, was born in Venezuela.

The steel-hulled *Simon Boliver* accommodates 194 persons, including 17 officers, 24 warrant officers, 102 midshipmen and 51 enlisted men, all of the Venezuelan Navy. The ship's beam measures 35 feet; her mainmast is 140 feet high.

Thomas Gillmer

Rediscovering the Past

The Ship Preservation Movement
Maritime Museums, Seaports and Restorations
Ship Models
Suvivors

The Ship Preservation Movement

Old sailing ships have been restored and preserved in many parts of the civilized world. In America, the move to save them has been sparked by a few crusaders whose enlightened followers have overcome the great expense and difficulties of finding and restoring historic ships, then moving them to places where they can be enjoyed by the public.

To admirers of Tall Ships it may seem obvious that these are works of art that deserve preservation as surely as examples of great works of architecture, great painting, or great sculpture. Beyond the artistry of their creation, the value of Tall Ships is that they illuminate our nation's history—our country's "roots." The world has lately begun to appreciate the full value of preservation. For years, a few men of vision could only rarely gather enough public attention to bring about the rescue of earlier ships. Building on public attention for historic sailing vessels and the sea, however, this movement is now gathering momentum.

The frigates *Constitution,* now at Boston, and *Constellation,* in Baltimore, are the best-known examples of what public contributions and demands for action made possible. Both are notable 18th Century sailing vessels, still floating. Year after year they draw crowds of eager visitors who pace their decks and marvel at the rigging with which sailors of old drove those wind ships through often unaccomodating seas.

As stars in the nation's earliest naval history, those two had special appeal. Many other worthy ships have not been so fortunate because of the failure to get all the necessary elements together at the right time—discovery, organization, publicity, enthusiasm and, perhaps most elusive of all, money for restoration.

Enthusiasm has flowered profusely in the past few decades as a band of global beachcombers search shores worldwide for deserving derelict ships. Museums celebrating sailing craft have multiplied and attracted more interest. Some enthusiasts are able to give financial help to the restoration efforts, some become hard-working volunteers, and the search and crusading goes on.

On the East Coast, among the earliest to recognize the value of ship preservation and the urgency of discovering candidates for restoration was Carl Cutler, a founder of the Marine Historical Society in Mystic, Connecticut. In 1936, Cutler published his classic book on clipper ships, *Greyhounds of the Sea.* In addition to working to compile records and save relics for the society, he started the process of saving the whaleship *Charles W. Morgan,* a wooden square-rigged vessel built in 1841, before the time of the clippers. *Morgan* ended her whaling career in 1920 at New Bedford, Massachusetts. For 15 years, a wealthy citizen of nearby South Dartmouth berthed the ship at his estate and took care of her. When he died, the ship decayed and a 1938 hurricane whipped her old hull into further deterioration. The society bought the ship and towed her to Mystic just before the United States entered World War II. There, the presence of the lovely old ship gradually broadened the scope of the society, which no longer limited itself to relics, records and models. This example of the economic validity of ship preservation, based at an institution devoted to marine history, gave other groups something to emulate.

In 1941, the same year that *Morgan* came to Mystic, young Karl Kortum signed on as a member of the crew of the last American-built square-rigged merchant vessel, *Kaiulani,* at San Francisco. She sailed the Pacific for a year before she was taken by the U.S. Army in 1942 to become a barge. At the end of the war she was hauling logs in the Philippines.

Kortum returned to San Francisco when the war ended. Campaigning for the creation of a maritime museum, he succeeded in interesting a newspaper editor and a wealthy collector of ship models. He managed to set up an exhibit in an abandoned waterfront building owned by the city, and from that slender start, he created what is now the National Maritime Museum. Meanwhile, he longed to save *Kaiulani* and suggested the project to Cutler. But Cutler thought he did not yet have the resources for so ambitious a project so far away, even though Mystic had acquired a second square-rigger, *Joseph Conrad.* The Mystic organizatioan was slowly becoming a new kind of maritime historical center—a seaport with real ships, supplemented by shoreside activities.

Kortum's museum had two floors of ship models. In 1954, he convinced his trustees to buy the square-rigged ship *Star of Alaska,* which had been built in 1886 as the British ship *Balclutha.* She was badly deteriorated but was restored at great effort the following year. This restoration, like the ones at Mystic, was extremely popular, earning large sums in admissions and swelling the restoration surge.

Following Cutler's precedent, Kortum added other ships to the floating attractions of the San Francisco museum. He acquired the lumber schooner *C. A. Thayer,* the steam schooner *Wapama,* the scow schooner *Alma,* and others. New life came to the San Francisco waterfront.

Because of his success with *Balclutha,* Kortum was invited to San Diego to help save *Star of India,* which was about to be scrapped. He surveyed the ship and wrote a report. Capt. Alan Villiers urged restoration, local fervor rose, and money was raised. The ship was fully restored and in 1970 was able to sail again, in better condition than she had enjoyed for years.

Kortum looked in distant places—even the Falkland Islands, a graveyard for many square-riggers. He located *Falls of Clyde,* an iron ship built in Scotland in 1878 and about to be scuttled in Seattle. A great effor was made to find a home for *Falls of Clyde,* for she is the only four-masted full-rigged ship in the world. (*Moshulu,* restored in Philadelphia, is a four-masted bark.) Kortum finally found a refuge for *Clyde* in Honolulu, and the mastless hulk was towed to Hawaii where she is a waterfront attraction.

An Australian was inspired to try to save the iron bark *Rona,* built in 1885 in Belfast, the last of a large number of sailing ship hulks in Australian waters. Fortunately, the Australian National Trust came to her rescue. Australia retrieved two other iron barks: *Polly Woodside,* in Melbourne, and *James Craig,* in Sydney.

A visitor to Kortum, fascinated with replicas, was convinced to shift his interest to an original ship and to start an effort to save *Kaiulani,* the vessel Kortum had sailed in years before. The result was the incorporation of the National Maritime Historical Society, which started out with the aim of bringing the ship to Washington, under sail, if possible. In 1964, she was given to the society by the Philippine people. Three years later, Congress authorized a loan to restore the last American square-rigger to carry cargo around Cape Horn. But the money never materialized and metal pirates raided the ship and stripped her. The sad end to the *Kaiulani* story is that only portions of the rudder skeg and forefoot were saved. These remnants are in storage, to be made part of a museum exhibit.

In 1967, the South Street Seaport Museum was founded in New York City, with Peter Stanford as its first president. That museum succeeded in raising funds to rescue an iron ship that had been rusting away in Argentina. The 2,100-ton *Wavertree* was built in England in 1885 as a cargo carrier. After being dismasted off Cape Horn in 1910, she spent her next 57 years as a barge in South America. The museum had her towed to New York in 1970.

It is taking years to restore the ship. Meanwhile, she is floating at her deck at the Seaport, visited by thousands of people each year and worked on by volunteers who respond to the posted plea: "Dirty work, long hours, no pay."

The nationwide interest in maritime history reached a high level in 1971, when the Sea Museum Council was organized by eight museums affiliated with the National Maritime Historical Society. In April of that year, the first issue of the society's magazine, *Sea History,* was published, with news of museums and ship restorations. The magazine continues to be the leading publication in the field of maritime history.

More individuals caught the ship preservation fever and became zealots. Peter Throckmorton, a marine archaeologist, spotted an old ship in Piraeus, Greece. He reported his find to Stanford, who put him in touch with Kortum, who was interested in bringing the ship to San Francisco. She was the British iron bark *Elissa,* built in 1877. Throckmorton mortgaged his house to raise the money to buy the ship and save her for later purchase by a museum. She was indeed saved and restored and was eventually brought to Galveston, Texas, where she is nurtured by a band of devoted volunteers.

Another handsome old ship was saved under the leadership of the Philadelphia Maritime Museum. An anonymous benefactor made it possible to restore and sail across the Atlantic the 157-foot wooden barkentine that is *Gazela of Philadelphia.* Well preserved, she still sails.

As the ship preservation movement has grown and has demonstrated time after time that ships draw people to the waterfront, both government and business have joined the movement for their own purposes—economic development, city revitalization and business opportunity.

Much of this is compatible with ship preservation, with museum enhancement and with re-creating an environment contemporary with the age of sail. It is imperative, however, that ship lovers be continuously vigilant to insure against the danger that the ships will be blanketed by rampant commercialism.

There are other ships and other places, here and abroad, enlivened by the ship preservation drive. In nearly all instances, the hard work and long haul of preservation are fueled by individuals of vision whose love of history, craftsmanship and sea adventure provide the enthusiasm required to inspire others. The resulting projects provide education and enjoyment for us all. They can be seen firsthand at historic locations throughout the United States and in foreign countries.

Baltimore/Maryland

Constellation

In 1794, pirates from the northern coast of Africa were raiding American ships in the Mediterranean. In response, the Congress of the new American nation called for the construction of six warships. Keels for three frigates were laid: *Constitution, Constellation* and *United States.* When a peace treaty with the Bey of Algiers was signed, work on the vessels languished. But in 1797, French privateers produced a new threat, and the three warships were quickly completed and launched.

All three frigates were designed by Joshua Humphreys of Philadelphia. Both *Constitution* and *Constellation* are still with us, located where they were built, the former at Boston, the latter at Baltimore. *Constitution* is the larger, displacing 2,200 tons to the 1,265 of *Constellation;* both are rigged as barks. *Constitution* was classed as a 44-gun frigate, *Constellation* as a 36-gun frigate. Actually, in her fighting days, *Constellation* carried 30, 24-pound carronades and 22, 42-pound carronades, and was operated by a crew of 368.

Of the three frigates, *Constellation* was the first finished, and therefore, technically is the oldest ship in the U.S. Navy. She also has a nickname—although not so famous as *Constitution's* "Old Ironsides". It is said that French sailors, impressed by *Constellation's* speed, dubbed her "Yankee Racehorse". She first went to sea in June, 1798, distinguishing herself on assignments for 157 years before being decommissioned and returned to Baltimore in 1955.

Constellation's first conquest at sea occurred in 1799, when she defeated the French frigate *L'Insurgente* in the West Indies. Early the following year, she out-gunned another French frigate, *La Vengeance.* In 1802, she took part in the Barbary Wars against Tripoli.

She fought in the War of 1812; in 1825, she was flagship of a West Indies squadron, chasing pirates. The ship sailed around the world in the 1840's. *Constellation* played a part in preventing the Hawaiian Islands from becoming a British protectorate, granting the emperor of Hawaii asylum aboard the ship when the British demanded his surrender.

In 1854, the warship was rebuilt, and she fought in the Civil War. *Constellation* is now the only warship surviving from that conflict. In 1871, she started taking midshipmen from the U.S. Naval Academy on summer cruises for sail training. She made her last trans-Atlantic voyage in 1892, carrying European works of art for the Columbian Exposition at Chicago.

Franklin D. Roosevelt, then Undersecretary of the Navy, recovered from a polio attack aboard the ship in 1926-27. She was later retired, but Roosevelt ordered her recommissioned in 1940, when he was President of the United States.

As a museum ship at Baltimore's Inner Harbor, *Constellation* is far from being a fully restored ship. Yet she is able to give visitors an accurate impression of the size, rigging and deck spaces of a sailing vessel of her size and age. She is 176 feet long, with a beam of 41 feet. Her anchor capstan, both on the main or spar deck and the gun deck clearly shows the strength required of working seamen.

The guns are in place on her gun deck. Unless you tap them and note the absence of a metallic sound, you would not know that many of them are fiberglass substitutes, installed to save weight and prevent further hogging of the hull. The keel is already out of line by about 20 inches at its ends.

Quarters for the officers and crew have not yet been restored and many other features are missing. Metal plates with inscriptions describe some features of the ship. Unfortunately, these are not well illuminated and are difficult to read. They were a gift to the ship.

Unlike *Constitution*, which is still in the U.S. Navy and is maintained as a Navy vessel with federal funds, *Constellation* belongs to the City of Baltimore, and is maintained on a slim budget based on admission fees and contributions.

Constellation was built of various woods, including live oak, white oak, yellow pine and Douglas fir. Her great bowsprit juts out over 67 feet; her mainmast is 170 feet high.

There has been some controversy about the authenticity of the ship. The present vessel is 10 feet longer than the original and has a round stern, whereas the original had a square stern. Some argue that the present ship was built at Norfolk in 1855, while others maintain the ship at Baltimore is the original, changed over the years. Supporters of that theory say that copper spikes dated 1797 have been found in the ship.

Contributions for maintenance and restoration of *Constellation* are being solicited by the U.S.F. Constellation Foundation, Constellation Dock, Baltimore, Md. 21202.

St. Michael's/Maryland

Chesapeake Bay Maritime Museum

One of the most charming of waterfront museums is the Chesapeake Bay Maritime Museum at St. Michaels, Maryland. This institution is entirely clear on its mission to collect, preserve and exhibit artifacts relating to the bay and the history of the people who have lived and worked on its extensive tidewater coastline. In carrying out that straightforward mission, this museum offers visitors a pleasant few hours among typical Chesapeake Bay watercraft and related exhibits in their lovely, languid, bayside background.

The St. Michaels installation is on a 16-acre peninsula created by masses of oyster shells predating the museum and constantly renewable for resurfacing paths and driveways. The peninsula juts out into the picturesque Miles river, one of the many deep and wide indentations that give the 200-mile long bay its ragged shoreline of more than 5,000 miles.

The most enticing building there, for the first-time visitor, is the hexagonal Hooper Strait Lighthouse, one of three remaining "cottage" beacons of many that used to light the way for bay mariners. First illuminated in 1879, this structure was moved to the museum from its original home further down the Chesapeake in 1966. Carefully restored, its three floors are authentically equipped and furnished, and are open for visitors' inspection.

Looking through the displays of equipment needed by the lighthouse keeper and reading pages of lighthouse keepers' journals are revealing. All romantic notions about the delights of lighthouse life are dispelled; it was lean and lonely.

The major attractions in the water at St. Michaels are examples of the most famous of Chesapeake Bay work boats, the skipjack and the bugeye. The skipjack is *Rosie Parks,* a centerboard boat whose single mast is sharply raked. The hull is shallow and has a V-bottom and hard chines. The bugeye is *Edna Lockwood,* a round-bottomed ketch with raking masts whose mizzen boom overhangs the stern. They are veteran oyster-boats. Both boats are painted white, including their decks, as if dipped in glossy whitewash, in the manner of bay work boats, and have no varnished parts. Neither boat may be boarded by visitors, but there's a lot of admiring that goes on from the dock.

Edna Lockwood is quite an old lady. She was built in 1886, rescued from decay about 1975, carefully restored, and re-launched in the late 1970's—a more dashing boat than she'd ever been as a working oysterer.

Rosie Parks was built in 1955 in Dorchester County with her sister oyster dredgers, *Martha Lewis* and *Lady Katie.* The latter is still working at Tilghman Island. *Rosie Parks* is 50 feet long on deck, 69 feet overall. Her draft is three feet with the board up, and she has 1,850 square feet of sails. Her mast is 65 feet above the waterline. Her owner was Captain Orville Parks, known as the unofficial "Admiral of the Chesapeake". He and *Rosie* won many skipjack races until he retired in 1975 after a 68-year water career. He died a year later at the age of 80.

The museum has a collection of historic work boats and day sailers on display, too. There are examples of canoes made by hollowing out logs, and of later log canoes constructed by joining logs together and shaping them. The museum also features a racing log canoe, a slender, over-canvassed sailboat that races on the Miles River in amazing exhibitions of acrobatic sailing. This is the most difficult to handle of all Chesapeake sailing craft, and sometimes the most exciting to watch.

Among day sailers on display is the first Comet, a class of 16-foot racing boats designed in 1932 by C. Lowndes Johnson of nearby Easton. The first Penguin is there, too. This is a class of 11.5-foot sailing dinghies designed originally for winter or "frostbite" racing by Philip L. Rhodes in 1939. Also in this museum is a Chesapeake 20 and a Hampton, two other classes of racing sloops popular on the Chesapeake in the 1960's and 1970's.

The museum has a fine collection of models and half-models of bay boats, including one of a pilot boat—a schooner that was a forerunner of the famous Baltimore clippers. Also on display are a model of a clipper of 1807 used for blockade running and one of an oyster dredging boat of 1882. Another piece of nautical nostalgia is a model of *Victory Chimes,* the three-masted schooner which sailed the bay as a cargo carrier in the early part of this century and can still be seen under sail.

In one of the museum's newer buildings there is an exhibit of decoys, from the crudest old working decoys to those works of art of today's craftsmen. And all around in the air and in the water are beautiful live examples of the neighborhood waterfowl—ducks, swans and gulls.

Annapolis/Maryland

U.S. Naval Academy Museum

A comprehensive collection of ship models is housed at the U.S. Naval Academy Museum at Annapolis, along with many other collections of paintings, photographs, prints, ships' instruments, flags, uniforms, manuscripts, rare books and other items relating to the history and traditions of the U.S. Navy. The museum has the Rogers Ship Models Collection of 108 models of sailing vessels from the period of 1650 to 1850.

Among the 108 are 17 Admiralty models constructed before proposed ships were built. There are 12 original British display cabinets of the William and Mary (1689-1702) and Queen Anne (1702-1714) periods. This collection is regarded as one of the most valuable of its kind in the world.

The museum originated in 1845 and has had its own building since 1939. It is open every day except for Thanksgiving, Christmas and New Year's Day, and there is no admission charge.

Maryland

Skipjacks

Years ago, there were about 1,500 skipjacks dredging oysters in the Chesapeake Bay. Perhaps two dozen now remain in this last fleet of work boats operating exclusively under sail in the United States. The skipjack is a sloop-rigged vessel, with a sharply raking mast, long boom and shallow hull with a centerboard and V-bottom. A few have been restored. One of those is the 80-foot *Flora Price,* owned by William Combs, which is seen on the Sassafras River and upper Chesapeake Bay as a pleasure boat. She was constructed in 1910 at Champ, Maryland, and has been restored to her original appearance.

Another restored skipjack is the 69-foot *Minnie V.* The shallowness of the typical skipjack's hull is illustrated by her dimensions. Although her length at the waterline is 45 feet, her draft with the centerboard up is only three feet. She is a 12-ton vessel. *Minni V's* home port is Baltimore, and she sails mostly on the Patapsco River during the warm months, taking school groups for half-day and full-day sails. She is owned by Ocean World Institute, Inc.

The working skipjacks in the oyster fleet have no engines because they are permitted to dredge only under sail power. They carry or tow yawl boats for use when they must resort to power.

Bath/Maine

Maine Maritime Museum

Four vessels at the Maine Maritime Museum at Bath are of interest to admirers of Tall Ships. Outstanding among these is the 142-foot Grand Banks fishing schooner, *Sherman Zwicker,* formerly at the Grand Banks Schooner Museum at Boothbay Harbor, also in Maine. She was built in 1942 in Lunenberg, Nova Scotia, carries 12 dories and has berths for 28 crew members. *Sherman Zwicker* is a fishing museum filled with gear and appurtenances of the prosperous days of plentiful fishing in this area in the 19th Century.

Browsing through a collection of equipment and pictures of life as it was for the hardy men who spent their working years aboard such ships helps to evoke a keener sense of their lives and times.

When she was launched, *Sherman Zwicker* was the largest fishing vessel in Nova Scotia's fleet. She usually made three trips to the banks from March to September, and in the cold months made cargo-carrying voyages to South America. Her crew fished with a trawl line a mile and a half long, with baited hooks every 10 feet. The line was tended three or four times a day by men in dories. The ship was referred to as a dory schooner and salt banker because of the use of dories and the method of preserving fish. Six of the dories were painted a maroon color and were stacked on the port side of the ship. The other six were buff-colored and were stacked on the starboard side.

Another vessel at Bath is *Maine,* a 53-foot pinky schooner, built by apprentices working at the museum, and launched in 1985. *Maine* was the first new wooden schooner to be launched there since 1920. She is a replica of a type of fishing craft used in New England and Nova Scotia in the 19th Century.

Many of the original pinkies were built at Essex, Massachusetts, and were pink-sterned, meaning each had a high, sharp stern with a narrow, overhanging, raking transom. They were two-masted schooners without topmasts (bald headed), and generally had a short bowsprit and one headsail.

The museum's fleet is also fortunate in having two examples of the Friendship sloops built in Maine in the early part of this century. These boats were made famous by the book *Princess,* revealing the love affair between the author, Joe Richards, and the Friendship sloop he rescued and sailed.

In 1985, the museum received a gift of *Iocaste,* a 1907 Friendship sloop, to be restored by the museum's apprentice shipwrights with aid from the Friendship Sloop Society. She joins *Chance,* a 1916 Friendship sloop designed by Wilbur Morse.

Built at Friendship, Maine, and nearby towns, these sloops were originally used for fishing, but in recent decades those remaining have become recreational sailers.

The museum at Bath sprawls over three sites on the Kennebec River, which makes a wonderful, watery setting for a visitor's exploration into the history of sailing ships. In addition to the museum's vessels afloat, there is the changing display of passing small craft.

The centerpiece of the museum is the Percy and Small Shipyard, which built more than 40 wooden vessels between 1896 and 1920. It is the only surviving shipyard in the United States where large wooden schooners were built. Its restored original buildings now house activities and exhibits that vividly recreate the marine history of a New England riverfront city. As the most expansive part of the museum, it is a busy place. One's imagination is aroused walking from building to building, being transported back to the years of careful construction with hand tools, through step-by-step explanation and illustration of wooden shipbuilding. From ship design and framing to planking and caulking, the working shops are eye-openers for the fiberglass sailor of today.

In one building, the history of the shipyard is traced. Another building houses the apprenticeshop, in existence since 1972, where young men and women are taught the traditional skills in wooden boat construction. The apprentices work with master shipwrights for 18 months to learn their craft.

One of the most fascinating exhibits at this museum is "Lobstering and the Maine Coast", which was opened during the summer of 1985. An extensive collection of lobstering gear, boats and photographs illustrates the lives of the lobstermen and their families from the age of sail to power. Some of the "galleries" that display the lobstering trade, from traps and boats to marketing, look like actual fishing shacks and canneries.

A special treat is a short film on lobstering, shown in a small theater that is a model of a lobsterboat. The late E.B. White, longtime Mainer, wrote and narrated the film, which recounts a day in the life of a lobsterman.

A boatride on the Kennebec River takes museum visitors to the other parts of the museum: the Sewell House, the only year-round segment, where there are exhibitions of navigational instruments and seafarers' memorabilia from all over the world.

A short walk leads to the third museum site, a former Congregational Church built in 1844. This is now home port for the "Life at Sea" exhibit, depicting living conditions on a 19th Century sailing ship. Also on display are marine art, ship models and many other shipbuilding-related objects.

Visitors arriving in their own boats can sail directly to the museum, which has guest moorings in the river.

Searsport/Maine

Penobscot Marine Museum

A fine collection of marine paintings is exhibited at the Penobscot Marine Museum in Searsport, Maine, a port on Penobscot Bay, downriver from the major lumber port of Bangor. The museum embraces a group of historic buildings containing exhibits on the age of sail, including one on the navigation instruments—quadrants, sextants, chronometers, logs—used in the 18th, 19th and 20th Centuries. Another illustrates the contributions of men and women of the Searsport area to the production of the square-rigged Down-Easters built in Maine to carry cargo on the oceans of the world.

The museum is open from Memorial Day until October 15.

Massachusetts

Peabody Museum of Salem

Founded in 1799 as the East India Marine Society, the Peabody Museum of Salem is the oldest continuously operating museum in the United States. In the 18th and 19th Centuries, marine societies were established to help dependents of deceased members and to collect observations and facts that would improve navigational knowledge. The far-sighted Peabody organization specified a third purpose in the charter of the Salem society: "To form a museum of natural and artificial curiosities".

Since membership in the society was limited to Salem sea captains who had "navigated the seas near or beyond the Cape of Good Hope or Cape Horn," a continuing supply of eclectic curiosities from remote parts of the world was assured.

Indeed, the captains seemed to enjoy bringing home assorted exotica, starting with amazing objects from India in 1803. Five Salem captains pooled resources to bring back several life-size portrait statues of Indian merchants with whom they traded, and a palanquin—a carriage designed to be borne by several men. Along with these items from India came costumes and gear for the carriage-bearers, and for some years, the whole Indian entourage was a colorful feature of an annual procession that paraded through Salem's streets, with East India Marine Society members appropriately costumed and geared. This Indian collection became part of the lives of the Salemites, who could visit it often inside the museum. In 1985, these large figures and all the appurtenances were completely refurbished to be part of a special exhibit, "Yankee Traders and Indian Merchants—1785-1865".

Figureheads in the East India Marine Hall, Peabody Museum of Salem   Photo by Mark Sexton, Peabody Museum of Salem

From the earliest collection, the museum has grown into three major departments: maritime history, ethnology and natural history. Maritime history is illustrated by ship models, paintings, portraits, marine prints, figureheads, scrimshaw, sailors' artifacts, navigational instruments and fishing implements. An unusual exhibit is a full-size reconstruction of the master's saloon from *Cleopatra's Barge*, America's first ocean-going yacht, built in 1816.

Among its many activities, the museum publishes "The American Neptune," a quarterly that is the oldest maritime history journal in the United States.

The museum has notable Asian collections consisting of textiles, carvings, pottery, jewelry, weapons, religious artifacts and household items, brought from Japan, China, Korea, Southeast Asia, India and the Himalayas. Porcelain, paintings, furniture and other wares obtained in the Orient in the 19th Century are displayed. While many of the treasures of this museum were brought back and presented directly by the Salem sea captain-members, the fine furniture, paintings and textiles came to the museum after having graced the homes of families of the Salem seafarers. In addition, there are carvings, clothing, weapons, tools and utensils from Indonesia, Polynesia, Micronesia and Melanesia in the Pacific Islands collections. The museum also has sculpture, masks and domestic objects in its African collection.

Another major area of interest at the museum is the natural history of New England, interpreted through a collection of plants, birds, mammals, fish, reptiles, amphibians and seashore life.

The Peabody Museum owns a collection of more than a million photographs, and its library preserves maps, charts, and manuscripts, in addition to books.

Early in 1985 Peabody Museum enlarged its already impressive collection of 5200 Chinese objects by merging with the China Trade Museum, which boasted almost 8,000 Chinese objects. A new Chine Trade Wing will open in 1987 to house the joint collection.

Salem, with its fascinating museum, is on Massachusetts Bay northeast of Boston.

Massachusetts

New Bedford Whaling Museum

Oil has been king at many places at many times. During part of the 19th Century, oil was king in New Bedford, Massachusetts, and the king's name was whale oil. New Bedford was the busiest whaling port in the United States in the 1850's when more than 300 whaling ships unloaded their barrels at that city's harbor.

The whaling heritage of the New Bedford area is preserved vividly in the Whaling Museum, in the historic district of the city. Anyone with only a short time to invest will profit by an authentic picture of that period in American maritime history. Children and adults return to the museum again and again to absorb its atmosphere of another age and to learn how hardy men in efficient small boats managed to capture the huge mammals of the sea.

An outstanding feature of the museum, duplicated nowhere else, is the exhibit that greets visitors as they enter. It is the whaling bark *Lagoda,* built in half scale— large enough for people to explore, small enough to fit inside the museum. Walking on the model and inspecting its faithful miniaturization of a whaling ship, one gets the feel of life on such a ship, and a clear impression of the gruelling labor, the crowded quarters and the ugly processes that whaling involved.

The gear used to tie up a dead whale alongside the ship is there, and one can picture the ship's officers cutting the blubber from the whale, standing over it on a narrow plank and wielding the long-handled knives. The try-pots where the blubber was rendered are reproduced on the same scale as the rest of the exhibit. Exploring the ship, one can easily relate its equipment to the processes of whale hunting and whale oil-rendering shown in detail in other exhibits. The only thing missing is the hideous stench that permeated the ships from stem to stern.

Equally revealing is a whaleboat crowded with its equipment—oars, a sail, harpoons, and the long, coiled rope with which the harpooned whale dragged the remarkably small boat and its courageous crew until the whale wearied. The many styles of harpoons are on exhibit, along with all other equipment that the whalers used to catch and dismember their prey. Whales, whaling, and assorted articles made from whale-parts are all covered in the many exhibits and shown in a film that can be seen periodically in the museum's theatre.

One of the most remarkable possessions of the museum is a panoramic painting, 8.5 feet wide and 1,298 feet long. This huge scenic painting, mounted on rollers, tells the story of a whaling voyage. It was painted in the 1940's by Benjamin Russell, a ship's carpenter on a whaler, and Caleb Purrington, a house painter in New Bedford. Panoramas were an art form of that time, and were shown to the public by being slowly unwound from one roller and re-wound on another, with about 12 feet of the painting always in view. A commentary on the story of the voyage accompanied the showing of the panorama, which was entitled simply, "Whaling Voyage." Because of Russell's observations and memory, the work depicts a wealth of detail on places the whalers went and on shipboard life of that period.

Directly across the street from the museum (which is at 18 Johnny Cake Hill) is Seamen's Bethel, the chapel of the sailing men. This is the Whalemen's Chapel of Herman Melville's "Moby Dick". Its pulpit is shaped like the bow of a ship, complete with a short bowsprit. Even in its simplicity, the chapel is an awe-inspiring place. The air is heavy with the atmosphere of the whaling age; more eloquent than the finest stained glass windows are the simple memorial plaques that line the small chapel's walls.

White-painted wood panels seem to surround the chapel visitor. Row on row, these plaques record in stark black lettering and unadorned language the names of the ships and the men lost at sea, with the dates of the marine disasters that ended their lives.

Massachusetts

Boston Tea Party Ship and Museum

Beaver II, a 110-foot brigantine, is a near-replica of one of the three British vessels boarded by angry patriots at Griffin's Wharf during the Boston Tea Party that triggered the American Revolution. The present vessel was built on the hull of a Baltic ship. Having sailed across the Atlantic Ocean with a symbolic cargo of tea, she is permanently moored at Griffin's Wharf at Boston as an exhibit at the Tea Party site.

The museum alongside the ship has exhibits portraying the political and economic conditions of the period just before the revolution, designed to help visitors relive the Tea Party rebellion and to understand its causes.

Constitution

Charlestown Navy Yard is a national park—part of the Boston National Historical Park. Its great treasure, in the eyes of Tall Ships enthusiasts, is the U.S.F. *Constitution*, the larger of the two oldest American warships still afloat. The other is the U.S.F. *Constellation*, in Baltimore. They were launched in 1797 and are still ships of the U.S. Navy. There are no better symbols of the nation's naval heritage and maritime tradition than these grand old frigates. There are also probably no clearer illustrations of wooden ships' need for constant maintenance and occasional restoration. *Constitution* is in excellent condition.

She is one of six frigates authorized by Congress in 1794, when the new nation was without a navy and American ships trading in the Mediterranean were being attacked by pirates from North Africa. *Constitution* was built at Boston, of wood selected from several locations from Maine to Georgia. Live oak used for her frames came from the sea islands of Georgia. The original keel is intact, and is part of the ten percent of the original ship that remains; the rest has been restored faithfully over the years.

Constitution is 204 feet long overall with a hefty beam of 43 feet, six inches. Her draft is 22 feet, six inches; she displaces 2,200 tons. The great ship has a mainmast 220 feet tall, and the sails on her three masts have an area of 42,710 square feet. She could move along at better than 13 knots.

A fighting vessel, *Constitution* carries 32 long guns with a range of 1,200 yards, 20 carronades with a 400-yard range and two "bow chasers", with a range of 1,000 yards. In her fighting days she carried a crew of 450. She also carries six boats ranging from 14 feet to 36 feet.

The bill for constructing this warship came to $302,718. In 1797 dollars, that would be equivalent to the cost of a naval ship today.

The first mission of the new vessel was to look for French privateers interfering with United States ships in the waters of the West Indies. Her deep draft was a hindrance in this effort; smaller ships were more effective.

Constitution's next major assignment was in the Mediterranean, where she served as flagship of a fleet that blockaded the port of Tripoli in 1803 and 1804. A peace treaty drawn up in the ship's cabin provided for an end to tribute to Tripoli and for the release of American captives.

Constitution's most historic exploits were made in the War of 1812, against England. Her first major victory was against the 38-gun frigate *HMS Guerriere,* near the Gulf of St. Lawrence. The U.S. vessel avoided firing until she was nearly abreast of the British ship, when the captain gave the order: "Now, boys, pour it into them!" Within 20 minutes, *Guerriere's* mizzenmast and much of her rigging were shot away.

The British vessel's bowsprit rammed *Constitution's* rigging and the crews of both ships tried to board their frigate foe for hand-to-hand combat, but the ocean was too rough.

The British managed to fire into the cabin of the United States ship and start a blaze that was quickly doused. When the ships separated, *Guerriere's* fore and mainmasts fell and her captain had to surrender. The Americans took the British crew as prisoners and burned the crippled ship. In the short battle—only 35 minutes —the British had 73 casualties, and the United States, 14. It was in that same battle that the British guns failed to crack the white oak planking of the *Constitution,* and one of the British tars is said to have complained, "Her sides are made of iron!" And that was how the ship earned the sobriquet, "*Old Ironsides.*"

She won a similar victory later over the 38-gun frigate, *Java.* In two hours, the British ship was dismasted and had surrendered. In 1815, "*Old Ironsides*" had her last great battle—against two smaller British ships, the frigate *Cyane* and the sloop *Levant.* She forced them both to surrender after a four-hour battle.

After the war ended *Constitution* was repaired, but in 1830 she was declared unseaworthy and was scheduled to be junked. Fortunately, Oliver Wendell Holmes' poem "Old Ironsides" stirred a surge of popular feeling, and funds were appropriated for rebuilding her in 1833.

The rejuvenated *Constitution* sailed around the world in 1844-45, covering

52,279 miles in 495 days at sea. The sailing frigate did not serve during the Civil War. She was rebuilt in 1878, and ended her sea-going duty in 1881. In 1905, when some of her wood was rotting, she was partially restored, and 20 years later she was fully renovated, with a large part of the funds coming from public subscription. The old warrior toured U.S. seaports from 1931 to 1934. She was overhauled again in the 1970's, when her copper sheathing was replaced.

Now she remains at her dock except on July 4th each year, when she makes her turnaround cruise and fires the national salute to celebrate Independence Day.

Visitors to "Old Ironsides" can explore the top deck, called the spar deck, go down to the second level, the gun deck, and see the "camboose" or galley stove where meals were prepared. The hand-operated bilge pumps are further aft, as is the anchor capstan, where the power of 75 men was applied to hoist the 5,300 lb. anchor. The captain's quarters, where several peace treaties were signed, are at the stern.

Down another level is the berthing deck, where the crew slept in hammocks. Visitors do not descend to the lowest of the four levels, the orlop, or hold, where the powder kegs were stored.

In 1985, Hurricane Gloria toppled a section of *Constitution's* fore royal, the top portion of the foremast. A long piece of Douglas fir was shipped in from the state of Washington for making the latest restoration on "*Old Ironsides*".

Across the pier from "*Old Ironsides*" is the USS Constitution Museum, which offers a history of the ship, exhibits that can be touched, and a simulated 1803 ocean crossing. Nearby, in the Navy Yard, is the building of the Boston Marine Society, with exhibitions of ship models, scrimshaw and marine art objects.

Another Tall Ship often seen at the Charlestown Navy Yard is *Spirit of Massachusetts,* the 125-foot schooner owned by New England Historic Seaport, Inc. The *Spirit* is based at the Navy Yard, but spends some time out sailing.

Newport/Rhode Island

Museum of Yachting

Close to the open sea at Newport, the Museum of Yachting is at Fort Adams, a state park. Opened in 1985, the museum has a brick building to house its indoor exhibits and a boat basin for its yachts. In 1986 the museum had the good fortune to be given $1.65 million by Thomas J. Lipton, Inc., with which to purchase *Shamrock V,* a J-Class sloop which competed in the America's Cup races in 1930. The yacht was entered by Sir Thomas Lipton, the Irish merchant who founded the tea company and who challenged for the America's Cup unsuccessfully five times.

Shamrock V is 119 feet long and her mast is 160 feet high. She is planked in mahogany over steel frames.

The new museum also owns the wooden yawl *Cotton Blossom IV,* built in 1926. The yawl has an overall length of 71 feet, three inches, and her mainmast is 86 feet high.

One of the indoor attractions at the museum is a photographic exhibit entitled "The Golden Age of Yachting" showing yachts of 1885 to 1914. The museum organization sponsors the annual Classic Yacht Regatta at Newport for boats built before 1952. The museum is open during the warm months only.

Mystic Seaport Museum

Mystic Seaport Museum is probably the best known maritime museum in the United States and its popularity is well-deserved. Started in 1929 as a small collection of maritime-related objects in one building, the museum has developed into the renaissance of a New England shipbuilding community.

Sprawled along the Mystic River just east of New London is a carefully accumulated collection of boats and ships and more than 60 historic buildings. The entire community is designed to illuminate the lives and times of the shipbuilders, ships and those who sailed them, as well as the industries and crafts that were part of Mystic's seafaring past.

It is fitting that the site of the museum was a thriving shipyard, one of several that prospered there in the 19th Century when Mystic was an important port. Whaling ships were built there and it was home for many whalemen. In the 1845-55 decade, when less than 1500 persons lived in the village, Mystic merchants owned 18 whalers. Local people are proud that clipper ships from Mystic made 11 percent of the fastest Cape Horn voyages between 1850 and 1860, and 22 clipper ships were built there.

Descendants of the local shipbuilding and seafaring families are still in the area. Some of their homes, other buildings and land are now part of the museum that brings us a rewarding re-creation of New England's maritime heritage.

Once inside the museum gate, the 20th Century is left behind. It is difficult to resist the temptation to explore the well-stocked museum store, near the entrance, until after you have explored the 18th and 19th Century buildings, ships and spirit of the Seaport.

Some of Mystic's early colonists were shipwrights who became land-lubbing farmers during the summer, but built sloops and schooners to sail to the West Indies as traders in the winter. From the 1600's, Mystic's life has been related to the sea.

Some of the buildings are on their original sites, others have been brought here and reassembled and some have been meticulously re-created by the museum, based on pictures of early buildings no longer in existence. Each is a typically New England structure and, where possible, houses exhibits related to the building's earlier use.

Mystic's first bank is here, with a shipping office on the second floor. There is also a cooperage, a mast hoop manufacturer's shop, a ship chandlery, an apothecary shop and more, all displaying appropriate relics of the 19th Century. The history of New England salmon fishing, oystering and lobstering are traced and explained in original or carefully replicated buildings that house the gear and appurtenances used by watermen. There is a 19th Century school, a chapel and a meeting house, ship models, and a model restoration shop where the models are kept in top condition.

The glory of the Seaport, however, is its treasury of sailing craft. The most prized possession is *Charles W. Morgan,* the only wooden whaler remaining from the large American 19th-Century fleet. Built in 1841 at New Bedford, she made 37 voyages on the Atlantic and Pacific in pursuit of whales until 1921. In her 80 years of whaling, she brought in 54,483 barrels of oil and 152,934 pounds of whalebone. These were in demand for candles, fuel lamps, lubricants, cosmetics, buggy whips, canes, corset stays and other objects.

A crew of 33 normally manned *Charles W. Morgan.* Visitors can see the narrow, crowded quarters in which they ate and slept on the ship, which is a three-masted bark displacing 313.75 tons. She is 106 feet, 6 inches in overall length and has a beam of 27 feet and a draft of 17 feet, 6 inches. Her mainmast is 113 feet high.

An unusual feature on *Morgan* is the gimballed berth in the captain's cabin, on the starboard side of the lower deck. It was installed in 1864, at the request of a master who wanted to convince his wife to accompany him to sea. All the officers and petty officers had quarters aft, while the crew was jammed into the forecastle, where there were berths for 20 men and barely enough space for their sea chests.

Between the officers' and crew's quarters on the lower deck is the blubber room. On the upper deck are the brick try works, in which the blubber was rendered. Seeing the great blubber hooks and the tackle used to hoist the large "blanket pieces" of blubber into the ship, one can visualize how the officers performed the arduous job of cutting the blubber.

Beneath the lower deck is the hold, where the barrels of whale oil were stored. All this can be seen by visitors who board the unique ship, and it is not hard to imagine the horrible odor that permeated the entire vessel.

After remaining in service longer than any other whaleship on record, *Charles W. Morgan* was acquired by Mystic Seaport and put in a sand berth in 1941. She was designated a National Historic Landmark in 1967, then re-floated in 1973. Restoration work was done at the Seaport's own preservation shipyard, another remarkable feature of the museum.

A second major floating attraction is *Joseph Conrad,* a full-rigged ship built in 1882 as a training vessel for cadets going into the merchant service of Denmark. Her original name was *Georg Stage,* in memory of the son of a prominent Danish shipowner.

The ship sank after being rammed by a freighter off Copenhagen. Raised and rebuilt in 1905, she was bought by Alan Villiers in 1934, and renamed for the famous seafaring author. With a crew of young people, *Conrad* made a voyage around the world that took two years. Later, she served as a private yacht for a time and then as an American training ship. She was donated to Mystic Seaport Museum in 1947 by an act of Congress. Here she serves as an exhibit vessel, training ship and living quarters for students.

Conrad is 110 feet, 6 inches in overall length and has a beam of 25 feet, 3 inches and a draft of 12 feet. Her mainmast is 98 feet high; displacement is 400 tons, including 103 tons of ballast in the form of 50-pound iron pigs in the bottom of her Swedish iron hull. She was able to do 12 knots with her 10,000 square feet of sail.

Joseph Conrad

The Mystic Seaport has a wealth of other sailing craft. One is *L.A. Dunton,* a Gloucester fishing schooner, 123 feet, 3 inches long, built at Essex, sold to Newfoundland owners in 1933. She came to the Seaport in 1940, where in 1963 extensive restoration work was done, including rebuilding her stern to the original design and replanking her topsides and some of her deck.

Another vessel at Mystic is *Regina M.,* a schooner built in Perry, Maine, in 1900. She is a double-ender of a type sometimes called the "Quoddy boat", and is pink-sterned.

An example of a sloop used on Long Island Sound for oyster dredging under sail is *Nellie,* built at Smithtown, Long Island, in 1891.

Mystic keeps the hulk of the schooner *Australia* as an exhibit of ship construction. She is 70 feet, 7 inches long and was built in Great South Bay, Long Island, in 1862. In 1962, the Seaport considered her for restoration but decided she was too far decayed.

Another schooner at the Seaport is the 61-foot *Brilliant,* built in 1932 at City Island, New York. At Mystic since 1953, she is used for sail-training.

Among other sloops in this collection are *Emma C. Berry, Estella A.* and *Annie. Berry* was built on the Mystic River at Noank, in 1866, of a design known as the Noank smack (today we would call her a cutter), with a large mainsail, two head sails and a gaff topsail. She was re-rigged as a schooner in the 1880's and was an active fishing vessel and freighter along the New England coast for many years. She was repaired many times, and in 1969, when she was 103 years old, she was given to Mystic Seaport. A major restoration project was finished in 1971. The museum has published an illustrated book on that work, *Restoration of the Emma C. Berry.*

Estella A. is a Friendship sloop built in 1904 in Maine, for lobsterman H.J. Ames, who named her for his daughter. *Estella* served as a workboat for nearly 30 years and then served time as a recreational craft. She was restored in Maine and is believed to be the most authentically restored Friendship sloop in existence.

Sloops like *Estella A.* were built at Friendship, Maine by Wilbur A. Morse, and in nearby towns by other builders. Similar in design to larger Gloucester sloops, which were as long as 60 feet, Friendship sloops were usually under 40 feet. They sported long bowsprits and were lightly built.

Annie is a sandbagger sloop built on the Mystic river in 1880. Racing boats of her type carried a tremendous amount of sail and were balanced by a crew of 12 or more, who shifted ballast by lugging 50-pound bags of sand from one side to the other as the boat tacked. These centerboard boats had exceptionally long bowsprits and long booms overhanging the stern. *Annie's* hull is 29 feet long, but she stretches nearly 70 feet from the tip of her bowsprit to the end of her huge boom and carries 1,313 square feet of sail. Boats of this type were raced on the Hudson River and in Long Island Sound from about 1855 to 1885.

Admirers of Tall Ships who also like to see beautiful small craft will find two sheds full at the Seaport, including Crosby catboats built on Cape Cod and various small yachts designed by Nathaniel Herreshoff, including his own famous sloop, *Alerion.*

The Preservation Shipyard, named for Henry B. duPont, a benefactor of the museum, is well equipped with an 85-foot spar lathe, a rigging loft, space where vessels may be brought indoors for repair work and a 375-ton lift. Visitors may watch from a gallery.

Among other Mystic features are a planetarium, a children's museum and an education program. In the museum's Mariner Program, young people 12 to 20 years old live aboard the *Conrad* while learning sailing, small boat safety, rowing, maritime history and related subjects. Those who successfully finish that basic course are eligible for sail training aboard *Brilliant,* which takes week-long cruises.

South Street Seaport Museum

New York City attained its prominence as a metropolis largely because of its position as a harbor close to the sea. During the first six decades of the 19th Century, much of its port activity was concentrated along South Street on the East River, where China clippers, coastal schooners, trans-Atlantic packets and other craft docked. South Street was known as the "Street of Ships." Later, this area declined and steamships used the Hudson River. Still later, steamships spread to other waterfront sites in nearby New Jersey and Long Island. Now the heart of the former South Street port area, at the foot of Fulton Street, has been preserved as a museum and seaport.

South Street has its own flavor, very distinct from that of any other seaport or museum complex because of its location. On the edge of, and to some degree entangled with the skyscrapers of downtown New York City, the early 19th Century waterfront is sharply contrasted with late 20th Century concrete and glass towers that, however anachronistic, provide a shockingly effective background for the tall masts and rigging of the old ships.

The Seaport museum has long piers extending into the East River to accommodate its collection of ships. Nearby, it has a series of restored buildings. Here are housed a fine bookstore, a gallery for permanent and special exhibitions, stores, workshops, a research library and other educational activities, its re-created 19th Century print shop and museum offices.

Of particular interest to Tall Ships buffs are the schooner *Pioneer,* the four-masted bark *Peking,* the full-rigged ship *Wavertree* and the fishing schooner *Lettie G. Howard.*

The *Peking,* built in Germany in 1911, is 347 feet long. Her first mission was to haul general cargo from Europe around Cape Horn to South America's west coast, where she was loaded with nitrates for fertilizer. The development of manufactured fertilizer put her out of that business. From 1931, she was used as a stationary training ship for a boys school in England. In 1974, she was purchased for the Seaport and she rests there at Pier 15. One of the films to be seen at the museum records a very stormy passage around Cape Horn in 1929 aboard *Peking.* This truly amazing film was made by Captain Irving Johnson, who managed to climb into the rigging with his camera to capture the action as wave after overwhelming wave rolled across the decks of the hard-pressed ship. His film portrays the agony of a Cape Horn gale more vividly than words can describe it.

Visitors get an excellent picture of life on a sailing ship by taking a guided tour of *Peking,* which is one of the last four-masted steel barks in the world.

Wavertree, built in England in 1885, has a hull of wrought iron, and is the largest sailing vessel with such a hull in any museum in this country. In her first few years, she was used to haul jute from East Pakistan (now Bangladesh) around the Cape of Good Hope to Great Britain. By 1888, however, she had to go into transporting general freight for long distances; steamships were preferred for shorter voyages. In 1910, *Wavertree* was dismasted in a storm off Cape Horn and spent the next 37 years as a floating warehouse in the Straits of Magellan, then about 20 years as a sand barge. The South Street Seaport obtained this ship of ill fortune in 1970, her iron hull still sound. Her decks have been rebuilt and her masts have been restored. Further restoration work is continuing on this century-old survivor of the seas.

The *Lettie G. Howard* was built of wood at Essex, Massachusetts, in 1893. She is 74 feet six inches long and is an example of the "Fredonia" type of fishing schooner that early in this century used to crowd into the Fulton Fish Market slip, where the Seaport is now. She was busy as a fisherman for 75 years before coming to the Seaport in 1968. When she is open, she has on board an exhibition of dory fishing and life on a fishing schooner in the early 1900's. Surrounding *Lettie G. Howard* and the other vessels are fascinating reminders of the busiest days of South Street's past, in libraries, old buildings, films, exhibits of crafts and other evocations of the "Street of Ships."

The Seaport frequently arranges workshops for adults, including instruction in model building for beginners and in making a ship in a bottle. Among the motor vessels at the Seaport is the sidewheeler *Andrew Fletcher,* on which visitors may take a 90-minute cruise in New York harbor, including a close look at the Statue of Liberty.

New York

Sag Harbor Whaling and Historical Museum

Sag Harbor, facing Shelter Island Sound at the eastern end of Long Island, was a major whaling port from about 1775 to 1871. It reached its height of activity in the 1840's, when there were 63 vessels in the whaling fleet. The Sag Harbor Whaling and Historical Museum recalls those days.

There is a whaleboat at one side of the museum's entrance, and on the other, the large kettles used in the try-works on whaling ships to boil the blubber and make whale oil.

Visitors entering the museum building, built in 1845 as the mansion of a whaling shipowner, walk through the jaw bones of a right whale. One room in the museum is devoted to harpoons and other tools and instruments used by the whalemen, along with log books of whaling ships. An original model of the bomb-lance, invented by a Sag Harbor whaling captain, is displayed. There are many examples of scrimshaw, that special craftwork of whalemen. The museum is open from May 15 until September 30.

New York

The Whaling Museum Cold Spring Harbor

A Cape Cod style building at Cold Spring Harbor, at the eastern end of Long Island, houses the Whaling Museum—a small museum with a broad educational program devoted to whales, whaling and maritime history.

This museum's permanent exhibit presents a chronological account of whaling based on Long Island. It traces whaling from the days when right whales were plentiful in the ocean off the.south shore of Long Island and were hunted first by native Americans and then by colonists until the decline of whale populations and whaling in the 19th Century. Cold Spring Harbor was one of the smaller whaling ports, with nine ships based there from 1836 to 1862.

The museum's education program reaches school children in all grades as well as adults. In addition to lectures supplemented by films, there are workshops on scrimshaw, sea chanteys, making a ship in a bottle, whale communication, and other whale and sea-related subjects. Films on whales, whaling voyages and conservation are shown in Sunday programs.

A whaleboat last used in 1913, a duplicate of those used in the 19th Century, is displayed at the museum. There are also harpoons, lances and other whaling implements to illustrate the methods used to capture those behemoths of the sea.

Philadelphia/Pennsylvania

Moshulu

The largest Tall Ship in the world is *Moshulu,* the four-masted bark tied up at the Philadelphia waterfront at Penn's Landing. At 393 feet, she is a few feet longer than the Soviet Union's *Kruzenstern,* the largest of the sail training vessels. The 1904 square-rigger has been well restored and is an outstanding museum ship.

Moshulu was built in Scotland for German owners and was originally named *Kurt.* During her first 10 years, she sailed mainly to Chile, bringing nitrates to Europe.

She was in Oregon to load a cargo of grain in 1914, when World War I broke out and she was ordered to stay there. In 1917, when the United States entered the war against Germany, *Kurt* was confiscated and renamed *Dreadnought.* Mrs. Woodrow Wilson, wife of the President, renamed her *Moshulu,* an American Indian word meaning fearless. The U.S. Shipping Board operated the vessel until 1921, when she was sold to an American company which used her to haul lumber for seven years. In 1935, she was sold to Gustav Erikson in Finland to be used as a grain hauler from Australia to Europe. She won the last grain race in 1939.

During World War II, *Moshulu* was confiscated by Germany and became a floating warehouse, with her spars removed. In 1968, a U.S. firm, Specialty Restaurants Corporation, bought this ship of many careers, had new spars made for her and brought her to the United States. The new owners spent more than $2 million restoring the bark and preparing for yet another career—as a combination museum and restaurant. In this role, *Moshulu* is a popular stopping place for waterfront visitors, who go aboard for refreshments and to admire her silhouette in the evening, when her rigging is outlined in white lights.

The museum aboard *Moshulu* has several attractions. In the master's and mates' quarters is a collection of photographs of the ship's entire sailing career, along with paintings and prints, a model of the ship, and exhibit of her tools, and a film, "Sailing with *Moshulu*." The restoration of the ship is also depicted in a slide presentation. Guided tours are provided.

Pennsylvania

Philadelphia Maritime Museum

One large room at the Philadelphia Maritime Museum at 321 Chestnut Street, Philadelphia, Pennsylvania, is devoted to Tall Ships. A showcase displays a sailmaker's bench and tools, including needles and fids of many sizes, as well as illustrations of the various stitches used by sailmakers. Another case exhibits the draw knife, adz, auger and other tools used by the shipwright. An informative mural depicts details of the rigging of a square-rigged ship of 1750, and another explores details of the mainmast and mainyard of an 1800 ship.

Also exhibited are models of historic sailing vessels. While most of them are wooden, there are several of bone or ivory made by French prisoners incarcerated in England during the Napoleonic Wars (1796-1815). These antique, all-white "prisoner-of-war" models are particularly interesting to examine. One bone model of *Caledonia,* a 120-gun ship of 1805, is more than four feet long.

A revealing exhibit for Tall Ships buffs is a model of a section of the 32-gun frigate *USS Essex.* The ship, 141 feet long, was active in the War of 1812. The open section reveals the construction and layout of a frigate.

A few blocks away the museum operates a "workshop on the water" consisting of a boat building shop and exhibits of small pleasure craft and work boats. Classes in old and new boat building methods are taught.

The museum also has "visible storage"—collections not on display may be seen as they are stored and preserved.

Other aspects of the mariner's world at the museum include marine art, navigational instruments, figureheads and scrimshaw.

Philadelphia/Pennsylvania

Port of History Museum

Thousands of years of the history of sail are exhibited at the Port of History Museum at Penn's Landing in Philadelphia. At the foot of Walnut Street on the Delaware River, this museum is a collection of wooden models of vessels that existed many centuries ago and of the Tall Ships that sailed more recently. The oldest ship represented is an oar-propelled Egyptian merchant vessel of the 13th Century B.C. A handsome double-ender with a bird's head at bow and stern, she was a long boat, using a square sail as well as oars.

A Roman merchant vessel of the Second Century A.D. is also part of the collection. A double-ended and beamy ship with square sails on two masts, the model also shows a mast tilting forward at the bow, perhaps a predecessor of the bowsprit.

Also on display is a three-masted English merchant ship of the 12th Century. Two of the masts carry sails; the third, at the stern, has a lateen rig. A Venetian galleass of the 14th Century had three masts, all lateen rigged, with 40 oars on each side.

Among several other models is one of a galleon of the *Mayflower* type, of the 17th Century, and one of *Welcome,* the ship which William Penn landed at New Castle, Delaware and Philadelphia in 1682. The model shows that she had three masts with square sails on two and a lateen rig on the last, and small square sails at the bow. She, too, was a galleon. A larger scale model at the Port of History Museum is of the six-masted schooner *Eleanor A. Percy,* built at Bath, Maine, in 1900. She carried coal, lumber and other bulk cargo along the East coast of the United States.

San Francisco/California

National Maritime Museum

One of the great museums of sea history is the National Maritime Museum at San Francisco, where nine ships have been preserved, including three Tall Ships. Five of the ships are classed as National Historic Landmarks. The museum, facing San Francisco Bay near the cable car turnaround, is in the Golden Gate National Recreation Area. The ships are at several piers along the waterfront.

To Tall Ships buffs, the most fascinating vessel in this marine assortment is the full-rigged ship *Balclutha,* built in England in 1886. She is typical of hundreds of sailing vessels of the 19th Century that struggled around Cape Horn to bring coal, wool, wine and other supplies from Europe and to buy grain in California for the return voyage. *Balclutha* is 301 feet long with a beam of 38 feet.

Another prize possession of the museum is *C. A. Thayer,* a three-masted schooner that was the last commercial sailing vessel operating from the West Coast of the United States when she retired in 1950. Built in 1895, *C. A. Thayer* at one time was among 900 vessels carrying lumber from the Pacific Northwest. Later she hauled salmon from Alaska and worked at cod fishing in the Bering Sea. *Thayer* is 156 feet long and has a beam of 36 feet.

The museum's third sailing vessel is *Alma,* one of the last San Francisco Bay scow schooners still afloat. She was launched in 1891. Her flat bottom and shallow draft enabled her to sail on the shallow waters of the bay hauling lumber, hay and other bulk cargo. She is 59 feet long and has a beam of 22 feet. *Alma* is a gaff-rigged schooner with a topsail on her mainmast overlapping the gaff.

Other ships in the museum's flotilla are a sidewheel ferry, an ocean-going tug, a paddlewheel tug, a steam-engined schooner, a submarine, and a Liberty Ship—all related to the bay's history.

In the museum building, there are exhibits featuring parts from San Francisco Bay vessels, ship models, marine artifacts and photographs. In a separate building, the museum has three research collections of books, oral history interviews, periodicals, manuscripts, log books, ship plans and historic photographs. The museum and its collections, including the ships, are administered by the National Park Service.

This is not only a remarkable museum because of its contents; it covers a large area physically as well as historically. Comfortable shoes for extended walking are recommended. Nearby Ghirardelli Square is an amazing example of city revitalization along the waterfront vicinity; the refurbished Cannery area is another lure, and the ships and ship-associated exhibits require lots of shank's mare activity.

San Diego Maritime Museum

The oldest merchant ship afloat is *Star of India,* built in 1863 on the Isle of Man in the Irish Sea, and now the pride of the San Diego waterfront. She is one of three historic large ships along the Embarcadero, all owned and preserved by the Maritime Museum Association of San Diego. The other two are *Medea,* an elegant steam yacht built in 1904, and *Berkeley,* a San Francisco Bay ferry built in 1898.

Star of India is a 1,197-ton iron ship, with a waterline length of 205 feet. Currently rigged as a bark, but originally a full-rigged ship, she was first named *Euterpe,* one of the Muses in Greek mythology. *Star of India* still carries the original figurehead of Euterpe, the Muse of music. In her early years, however, *Euterpe* was not music to the ears of her owners. On her first voyage from Liverpool to Calcutta she collided with a Spanish brig off Wales and had to return for repairs and to replace crew members who took part in a mutiny. She then made it to Calcutta and back. But on her second trip, which started on New Year's Eve of 1864, *Euterpe* was hit by a cyclone in the Bay of Bengal. Her three masts were cut away to keep the ship from floundering. After a long delay, she was re-rigged at Calcutta. Ten days out of port, on her way home, the captain died of a tropical fever. It was nearly two years before she got back to Liverpool, where her owners sold her.

Euterpe made four more voyages to India and then carried cargo and emigrants to New Zealand and Australia, returning to England by way of Cape Horn, making 21 circumnavigations.

In 1901, the ship was sold to the Alaska Packers Association of San Francisco, who re-rigged her as a bark by removing square sails from the mizzen. Accommodations were built for 200 fishermen and cannery hands. She then made 22 annual voyages to Alaska in the spring and back to San Francisco in the fall.

In 1906, her owners changed the ship's name to *Star of India* to coincide with the names of their other ships, all "Stars" of various places.

In 1918, she had a close call, narrowly escaping being driven ashore by ice in Alaska, where she was frozen in. Her crew watched helplessly as another windjammer was pushed onto the rocks and wrecked. *Star of India* made her last voyage for the packers in 1923. She seemed headed for use as a storage hulk or some other ignominious end when she was rescued by a benefactor who bought her and gave her to the Zoological Society of San Diego in 1926, with the idea of making her a different kind of star as a floating aquarium and museum. But money for the conversion was not forthcoming, and the ship deteriorated. Eventually she was turned over to the new Maritime Museum Association of San Diego, which hoped to restore her. That hope got a gigantic boost in 1957 from Captain Alan Villiers, author and sailor of square-rigged ships. *Star of India* was fully restored and put to sea again under full sail, at the age of 113 years, in 1976 in honor of America's bicentennial.

Now, her onboard exhibits give visitors a picture of the working history of this ship. She is in sailing condition, and volunteers are trained to help handle her under the direction of experienced sailors.

Star of India's main yard measures 72 feet, and her jibboom is 55 feet. The vessel has a beam of 35 feet and her mainmast is 124 feet, eight inches high. She draws 22 feet when loaded.

For the museum on the ship, docents are available to guide visitors on tours, and there are also cassette tapes for self-guided tours. A gift shop offers scrimshaw, ship models, books and other articles.

Other features of the San Diego Museum include a collection of ship models and a library.

Washington, D.C.

National Museum of American History

A vivid overview of the history of sailing vessels in America is shown in half and full models in one of the museums of the Smithsonian Institute in Washington, D.C. On the first floor of the National Museum of American History, the maritime exhibit provides an informative and pleasant browse for Tall Ships buffs.

A few of the models are large. One of those is of the *Mayflower,* showing her 17th Century rig with a lateen sail at the stern and a square sail on the bowsprit in addition to her other square sails. (A 20th Century touch here may jar the purist: the sails seem to be Dacron.) Even larger than the model of the galleon that brought the Pilgrims to Plymouth is a model of the full-rigged ship *Brilliant,* built in 1775. She hauled tobacco to Liverpool and was taken over by the British after the outbreak of the American Revolution.

Sailing enthusiasts will be particularly interested in the National Watercraft Collection, an exhibit of 29 models, showing sailing craft at various periods in American maritime history. There are also many half models of hulls. Among the ships illustrated in models of high quality are clippers of the 1850's.

There is a model of *Tillie E. Starbuck,* the only full-rigged American ship made of iron and steel. She sailed from New York to Portland, Oregon, in 106 days, a record never bettered. The ship was built in Chester, Pennsylvania, in 1883 and was wrecked off Cape Horn in 1907.

Another showcase is filled with revealing models illustrating the development of New England fishing schooners from the traditional bluff-bow of the early ships to the slender bow of *Fredonia,* the Edward Burgess design of 1899. Burgess' style was widely copied, making commercial fishing more efficient by increasing the speed of the ships.

Filling a niche-like gallery is a whaling boat, full size, so loaded with harpoons, lines, oars and other equipment that there is little room for the crew. Here, the visual background, a mural of ships and whaleboats in a raging sea, and the sound, a medley of sea-chanteys, beguile the visitor into considering again the perilously difficult occupation of the whalemen.

Another of the many exhibits in this museum features the oldest surviving American warship–the little sloop *Philadelphia,* built in 1776 for the Continental Congress. She was one of a fleet of gunboats built for use on Lake Champlain to battle the British under General Burgoyne. *Philadelphia* was sunk in the fighting in October, 1776.

In 1935, the sloop was discovered on the lake bottom, by a diver. She was hoisted and later acquired by the Smithsonian, to become part of an exhibit on American naval history. The cannonball that sank her is also on display, and the hull still has the hole that cannonball made.

The sloop was made of wood. The hull is 53.3 feet long and the beam is 15.5 feet. The flat-bottomed sloop, which carried three guns, drew only two feet.

Other exhibits show what a waterfront warehouse looked like in 1776 and an illustration of the rigging of square-rigged ships. There are also many lithographs of ships and port scenes.

Charleston/South Carolina

Behemoth

Behemoth is a 65-foot gaff-rigged schooner built as a Chesapeake Bay oyster dredger of the 19th Century. She is unusual since most of the sailing vessels in the oystering business of that day were the traditional skipjacks and bugeyes, a few of which remain as work boats still bringing in the treasured oysters. Restored by volunteers, *Behemoth* sails from her base in Charleston, South Carolina.

She has a 13-foot beam and a draft of four feet six inches. Her rig is 56 feet high and she displaces 15 tons. She takes passengers on cruises.

Newport News/Virginia

Mariners' Museum

The place to see figureheads from ships of the past is the Mariners' Museum at Newport News. It has the world's largest collection of examples of the woodcarvers' art that used to ornament the bows of sailing vessels and seemed to help prop up their jutting bowsprits. Many of the sizeable square-rigged school ships proudly wear their figureheads today. Those at the museum were salvaged from ships that ended their sailing lives long ago.

The museum also has a fleet of miniature ships; among them are models of *Constitution* and *Constellation.* There is an extensive library of books on marine subjects and a huge file of photographs.

This museum arranges special, changing exhibits. An example is one on "Christmas at Sea", which shows the hard life of the crew aboard sailing ships of the early 19th Century. Here is displayed the crowded, dingy forecastle, where the sailors ate, slept and spent their off-duty time—their dog-watch and liberty days, when the ship was at sea. The exhibit illustrates the decidedly unromantic decor of narrow bunks, closely cluttered sea chests, boots and oilskins in the poorly-lighted area near the bow of the ship that was home to the crew.

Detroit/Michigan

Dossin Great Lakes Museum

The Dossin Great Lakes Museum is the marine branch of the Detroit Historical Department, with a building on Belle Isle in the Detroit River. Among its offerings is the largest collection in existence of models of Great Lakes ships. All built on a uniform scale, they trace the development of water transportation from birchbark and dugout canoes, through the era of sail, to steam and Diesel-powered ships.

Included in the sailing craft models are *Griffon,* which in 1670 was the first sailing vessel on the lakes, and *Niagara,* Commodore Oliver Hazzard Perry's flagship in the Battle of Lake Erie in the War of 1812. Another is *David Dows* which, in 1881, became the only five-masted schooner built to serve on the lakes.

Among the steamship models is the *City of Detroit III,* built in 1912. She was the sidewheeler that was the queen of the Detroit & Cleveland Navigation Company's fleet. Visitors to the museum enter the smoking lounge of the palatial sidewheeler, restored and preserved with its huge, three-panelled stained glass window and its hand-carved decorative woodwork. When the ship was built, she was the largest sidewheeler in the world, and this lounge was her showpiece. It is an outstanding example of "Steamboat Gothic" architectural style with its exquisitely carved Gothic arches and tracery reminiscent of the delicate stone carving in cathedrals.

Friends of the Tall Ships will be especially interested in a display of antique navigational instruments, an exhibit of shipbuilding tools and one of half-models. A topographical model of the Great Lakes helps to establish the background for the museum's depiction of the maritime history of the region.

Great Lakes Historical Society

The Great Lakes Historical Society at Vermillion, Ohio, on Lake Erie, preserves and interprets the maritime history of the Great Lakes. It operates a museum with a bountiful collection of ship models, marine relics and artifacts, paintings and photographs. It also houses one of the largest collections of marine engines in the United States.

Among the displays in the museum is one of the tools used in building wooden ships. There are several operating exhibits and re-creations of portions of ships.

The displays and pictures at this two-story museum recall the maritime history in which thousands of ships were built and sailed on the Great Lakes, carrying passengers, timber, minerals, and grain.

One of the models here is of *Niagara,* Commodore Oliver H. Perry's flagship in the Battle of Lake Erie in 1813. Timbers from the ship are also on display along with other artifacts.

Greenwich/England

Cutty Sark

The only 19th Century clipper ship still surviving is the famous and beautiful *Cutty Sark,* built in 1869 for the tea trade with China. The name comes from the Robert Burns narrative poem, "Tam O'Shanter." "Cutty Sark" refers to short-skirted Nannie, the devilish wench who deprived Tam's horse of her tail as she tried to get her rider across a stream after Tam tarried too long at the tavern. Nannie is *Cutty Sark's* figurehead.

The builders of *Cutty Sark* designed her to triumph over *Thermopylae* in the tea races, but she did not succeed. On her first voyage from Shanghai to London in 1870, Cutty Sark brought her cargo home in 110 days; her rival managed it in 105.

The black-hulled beauty has a double line of gold leaf emphasizing her graceful sheer line. She is a wooden ship with iron ribs, and her decks are solid teak. A long, slender clipper, she is 282 feet in length, and her beam is only 36 feet. She displaces 2,133 tons and has a draft of 21 feet. Her rig is 150 feet high; her sail area is nearly 32,000 square feet.

Cutty Sark worked profitably for about 15 years hauling tea from China and wool from Australia to England. In 1895, she was sold to a Portuguese owner for service in the Atlantic.

She was a clipper said to be a "happy ship", loved by all who sailed on her. Under the Portuguese flag, her name was changed to *Ferreira;* she was referred to fondly by her crew as "El Piquina Camisola", a translation of Scots' Cutty Sark.

Wilfred Dowman, an English captain, bought the clipper in 1922 and restored her fully to her classic loveliness. Thanks to him, this last clipper survives. She is in dry dock at Greenwich, where she provides a remarkable example of living maritime history.

Portsmouth/England

Mary Rose

Mary Rose, built in 1511, was the flagship of King Henry VIII's fleet. She sank off the coast of England in 1545 and her remains were hauled up from the mud a few years ago. The starboard side of the hull is remarkably well-preserved. The sterncastle remains, but the forecastle has disappeared. The resurrected ship is being preserved as a museum ship and will not be restored. She can be seen at Portsmouth, where *Victory* is in dry dock.

Many artifacts from the ship have been retrieved and are in a nearby museum where they give a view of 16th Century shipboard life. Some of the cannons from the ship were recovered long ago and are in the Tower of London.

Mary Rose is believed to be the first warship to have gunports cut in her topsides. But they were cut too low—only 16 inches above the waterline. So she sank in the same way *Vasa* did in Sweden—by taking in water through her open gunports when she heeled.

Portsmouth/England

Victory

There have been at least five British ships named *Victory.* The one preserved in dry dock at Portsmouth, England, was launched in 1765 after six years of construction. She is the ship on which Lord Nelson was fatally wounded during the Battle of Trafalgar in 1805. On the anniversary of the battle each year the ship's signal flags are raised with Nelson's famous message: "England expects that every man will do his duty."

Victory is a first-rate ship of the line, carrying 102 guns on three decks. Her keel was built of elm 18 inches thick, and her frames are of English oak. The planking of Baltic oak is in three layers, each five inches thick. Her bottom is lined with 17 tons of copper sheets. She displaces 3,500 tons and carried a crew of 850. She is a full-rigged ship.

Victory is 226 feet six inches long from figurehead to stern, has a beam of 52 feet and a draft of 25 feet. Her mainmast towers 205 feet above the deck. She has been well restored and preserved.

The J-Boats

During the 1930's, for the 14th, 15th, and 16th defenses of the America's Cup, the boats used were in Class J, defined in the Universal Rule of Measurement. They were large yachts, from 119 to 135 feet in overall length, carrying about 7,500 square feet of sails. They were known as sloops at the time, but we would now call them cutters, because each had two or three headsails. These boats were the first America's Cup yachts not to have gaff-rigged mainsails. Instead, their designs switched to the triangular mainsail and tall marconi rig—which got its name from the high radio antenna masts of the period, introduced by Guglielmo Marconi.

Ten J-boats were built on both sides of the Atlantic for these contests; from those, the six challengers and defenders were chosen. In 1930, *Enterprise* defeated the challenger, *Shamrock V,* the last of the series of unsuccessful challengers brought to America by Sir Thomas Lipton. In 1934, the defender *Rainbow* held off *Endeavor.* Finally, in 1937, the American yacht *Ranger,* believed to have been the fastest J-boat ever built, won the series in four straight races, downing *Endeavor II.*

The J-boats never raced after 1937. The American boats were all scrapped and their lead and bronze were salvaged. In England, however, most of the J-boats were kept afloat. At least three of the long, graceful J's have been or are now being restored.

Shamrock V, of the 1930 races, and *Velsheda,* which never had the honor of being the cup challenger, are back in the water in more than their original glory. In the

1930's, these were giant daysailers, built strictly for racing. Now they are cruising yachts with proper accommodations, but still with their traditional beauty as the elegant racing yachts of half a century ago.

Endeavor II was being rebuilt rather than restored in 1985-86, with her riveted steel hull being replaced by a welded one. There is little left of the original, which had been owned by T.O.M. Sopwith. An elegant cruising yacht of majestic size, the new 165-ton J-boat was designed to be 130 feet long, with a beam of 22 feet and a draft of 15 feet. Her aluminum mast towers 165 feet above the water.

The yacht still has the seven-eighths cutter rig she had in 1937. That means the headstay is attached seven-eighths the way up the mast, rather than at its very top. A jib is set on that stay and a staysail flies on another. Hydraulic winches help raise a mainsail with an area of 4,822 square feet.

The spinnaker has an area of 13,000 square feet. Also part of the new design is a 200-horsepower engine and bow-thrusters to assist in getting away from docks, or in pulling up to them.

In 1986, at least, *Endeavor II* may well be one of the most grandiose yachts under sail.

Ship Models

Model of HMS Marlborough of 1708, from the Krigstein Collection. The Krigstein Collection

Many individuals who are fascinated with the sea and ships get great pleasure from making or owning historic ship models. This is a hobby that people have enjoyed for hundreds of years, and one that probably has more adherents today than ever before.

Most model builders who are not professionals start with kits of pre-cut parts. There is, of course, a great range of quality among the kits available. Those made of plastic are the easiest to assemble and the least expensive but are also the least realistic and the least detailed. Several firms offer kits for wooden models based on authentic designs, with walnut or other hardwood for planking and metal parts such as rudder hardware and mast caps, made of brass and bronze. A moderately skilled modeler can transform such kits into finely detailed ship models of considerable beauty after many hours of absorbing work.

Some professional and amateur builders spurn the kits, even those of high quality, and insist on building their ships from scratch. The professionals build their models for sale and find a market among museums, people who have private collections of ship models, and others who like to own one or two handsome models to ornament their homes. There are not only professionals who build ship models, but others who sell, appraise, purchase and restore them, particularly those considered to be of museum quality.

Firms that sell kits and the various professionals concerned with ship models can be located through advertisements in such publications as *Sea History* and *Sea Heritage News.*

Perhaps the most lavish ship model ever built is a sterling silver rendition of the 19th Century clipper *Cutty Sark.* The four-foot ship glistens with 33 silver sails on her three silver masts. The scale is three-sixteenths of an inch to one foot. This model, created by a master silversmith in England, belongs to a private British collector.

There is also a sterling silver model of *Flying Cloud,* one of the clipper ships designed and built by Donald McKay. The record for the fastest voyage of a sailing ship from San Francisco to New York is 89 days and 21 hours, and is held by *Flying Cloud.* This silver model, crafted in the United States by Reino Martin, is the perpetual trophy used for the Donald McKay Race for sail training ships. The winner's name is engraved on the trophy.

Model of Wanderer at the Peabody Museum of Salem

Photo by Mark Sexton   Peabody Museum of Salem

Among collectors' prize possessions and museum pieces in this field are models made of bone or ivory. Many such models were made by French prisoners in British jails during the Napoleonic Wars, and are known as "prisoner-of-war" models. Examples may be found in private collections and in museums, including the Philadelphia Maritime Museum.

Several maritime museums have excellent collections of models. The Mariners Museum at Newport News, Virginia, has more than 1,000 models that trace the development of water transportation. The world's largest display of ship models built to a uniform scale is believed to be at the Dossin Great Lakes Museum at Detroit, Michigan. The National Museum of History and Technology, part of the Smithsonian Institution in Washington, D.C., has more than 175 splendid ship models showing the evolution of American shipping.

Among the rarest and most precious of ship models are those not constructed as miniature reproductions of existing ships or ships of the past, but scale models used in designing the ships before the days of blueprints and technical drawings. In England during the 17th and 18th Centuries, meticulously detailed "Admiralty Board" or "dockyard" models were submitted to the Lord High Admiral and the Navy Board when a new warship was proposed. Modifications were agreed upon after examination of the model and before construction began.

Admiralty Board models are remarkable, rare antiques—artistic creations crafted long ago for an important utilitarian purpose. One can visualize the admirals inspecting the superbly detailed, precise models and discussing the hull shape, the rigging, the placement of the guns.

There is a collection of Admiralty Board models in the National Maritime Museum at Greenwich, England. In America, nine of them are in the world's largest private collection. Called the Krigstein Collection, it contains four 17th Century and five early 18th Century models. Another prize in this little-known collection is the oldest ship model display cabinet in existence, built in the decade of 1670 to 1680. In the gilded cabinet is an Admiralty Board model of a 36-gun ship built during the reign of Charles II (1660-1685).

One treasure in the Krigstein Collection was built in 1702 for the construction of *HMS Warspite,* a 70-gun ship. A crowned, gilded lion is at the bowsprit of the model, built to a scale of one-quarter inch to the foot. This model was for 270 years in the family of the Earl of Pembroke, who was first Lord of the Admiralty in 1701.

Three of the models were obtained from the collection of J.P. Morgan. One of those was built in 1695 for the construction of *HMS Coronation,* a 90-gun ship. The scale is one-quarter inch to the foot. Another of the models was built prior to construction of *HMS Lion* in 1710. The 64-gun ship was 144 feet long and displaced 906 tons. The model shows a gilded lion figurehead on a curved bow with no bowsprit. The stern is also gilded and is topped by three lanterns.

A model of the 90-gun *HMS Marlborough,* built in 1708, has a complex figurehead showing John Churchill, first Duke of Marlborough, mounted on a horse and trampling an enemy. The scale is one-sixth inch to the foot.

The Krigstein Collection also has a "prisoner-of-war" bone model of *HM Frigate Pallas,* a 32-gun ship built in 1804. The oldest model in the collection is of a mid-17th Century Dutch three-masted vessel.

Among other exquisite rarities in this collection are two tiny models of early ships built by D. McNarry, to the scale of one inch equalling 16 feet.

One of the greatest public collections of admiralty models is at the U.S. Naval Academy at Annapolis, Maryland, where there are 17 such models and 12 display cases from the late 17th and early 18th Centuries. At this museum the public may see the Rogers Ship Models Collection, containing 108 models of ships that sailed from 1650 to 1850.

The best ship models involve considerable detail, as does this bow section of a 70 gun ship built in 1702.

Sea Serpent model, circa 1850.

Survivors

Each of the following sailing vessels is the last survivor of a type or is unique in some way:

Oldest fully restored iron merchant sailing ship: *Star of India,* at San Diego, California.

The only bark-rigged private yacht in existence: *Sea Cloud,* now a cruise ship.

The only surviving ship built to maintain submarine cables: *Western Union,* a youth training vessel.

The largest iron sailing vessel surviving: *Wavertree,* at South Street Seaport, New York.

The oldest surviving American warship: the sloop *Philadelphia,* built in 1776, now indoors at the National Museum of American History, Washington, D.C.

The oldest and largest wooden square-rigger still able to sail: *Gazela of Philadelphia.*

The largest sail training vessel: *Kruzenstern,* the U.S.S.R.'s four-masted bark, 378 feet long.

The first ocean-going warship armed with heavy guns inside her hull: *Mary Rose.* The starboard half of the salvaged 1510 ship is at Portsmouth, England.

Only fully restored Grand Banks fishing schooner built in New England: *L.A. Dunton.* At Mystic Seaport, Mystic, Connecticut.

Last full-rigged ship to go around the world under sail: *Joseph Conrad,* at Mystic Seaport.

Last fishing schooner of the Fredonia type: *Lettie G. Howard,* at South Street Seaport.

The only surviving clipper ship: *Cutty Sark,* now a museum ship at Greenwich, England.

Oldest commissioned sailing vessel in the U.S. Navy still floating: *Constitution,* at Charlestown Navy Yard, Boston.

Last American Grand Banks fishing schooner continuing to sail: *Adventure,* built in 1926; carries passengers from Camden, Maine.

Only surviving San Francisco Bay scow schooner: *Alma,* at the National Maritime Museum, San Francisco.

Oldest intact unrestored ship in North America: *Alvin Clark,* built in 1846, foundered in 1864, raised from Lake Michigan in 1969, now a museum ship at Menominee, Michigan.

Last surviving ship for whaling under sail: *Charles W. Morgan,* at Mystic Seaport Museum.

Only restored four-masted, full-rigged ship: *Falls of Clyde,* at Honolulu, Hawaii.

Largest Tall Ship in the world: *Moshulu,* four-masted bark, with sparred length of 393 feet, now a museum ship at Philadelphia, Pennsylvania.

History
Comes
Alive!

Replicas
Apprenticeshops
Shipbuilding and restoration projects

Famous Replicas

Many replicas or near-replicas of revered ships of the past have been built in recent decades as appreciation and understanding of American seafaring history has increased. In this section, we report on some of the more interesting replicas that Tall Ship enthusiasts will enjoy seeing.

No attempt is made to distinguish between true replicas—exact in all details—and the near-replicas which look like the originals, but may have been modified in many hidden but important features of construction. A replica built to sit quietly outside a museum and never go to sea could be built to be an exact duplicate of the original. However, replicas intended to sail on the ocean with passengers must meet modern standards of safety at sea that the originals could not meet today. One can therefore expect watertight bulkheads and whatever modification it takes to insure stability in replicas intended to sail with passengers. These and other safety features were never in the original ships.

Skillfully crafted replicas, built by oldtime methods, look like the originals, and are a delight to behold, and in some cases, to board for a taste of sailing as it was long ago. When one sails on *Sea Lion*, for example, the pleasure and excitement at stepping on a 16th Century square-rigged vessel that actually takes passengers is undiminished by the knowledge that the ship may sail legally with passengers on inland waters but would not meet current standards for an ocean voyage.

Some replicas are built to sail with their crews, but not to carry passengers. Examples are *Dove* and *Pride of Baltimore*. Others are built mainly to be part of a re-creation of an old waterfront scene. An example is *Globe*.

In all cases, replicas are living history. They bring to life a significant part of the history of the nation and the world that no words, paintings, photographs, film or television re-enactments can equal. They show us in their unique way: this is how it was.

Stanley Witkowski, Jr., Dupont Co.

BLUENOSE II
CANADA

The 160-foot gaff-rigged schooner, *Bluenose II* is a replica of the famous Grand Banks fishing schooner of the same name, pictured on the Canadian dime.

The original *Bluenose* won many of the International Fishermen's Races in the 1920's and 1930's, competing with boats from New England. The replica was built in 1961 in Lunenburg, Nova Scotia, in the same yard that built the original. She is used for charters and for public cruises. The vessel normally carries three officers and 10 crew members, and her home port is Lunenburg. She carries 12,550 square feet of sails and has a beam of 27 feet. She gracefully combines large size and beauty under sail with her 125-foot rig. To many people the Nova Scotia schooner is the epitome of the classic schooner and *Bluenose II* is the well-loved living example.

Norman J. Brouwer

BILL OF RIGHTS
UNITED STATES

A wooden replica of an 1856 schooner, *Bill of Rights* is 151 feet overall. She was built at the Harvey Gamage yard in South Bristol, Maine, and is gaff-rigged, with topsails. Her home port is Newport, R.I., where she works as a passenger-carrying vessel. The 99.8 ton schooner has 6,300 square feet of sail and her rig height is 115 feet.

BOUNTY II
UNITED STATES

At least two replicas of the 18th Century *Bounty* have been built for use in motion pictures based on the famous mutiny of 1789. A replica was constructed at Lunenberg, Nova Scotia, for the MGM film and was sailed more than 7,000 miles to Tahiti, where the filming was done. For once, a sailing ship did not have to fight her way around Cape Horn! Instead, she went quietly through the Panama Canal.

Bounty II is a full-rigged ship; on her mizzen are three square sails and a spanker. She has 18 sails on her three masts, and her total sail area is 10,000 square feet. The 480-ton ship is 118 feet long. More than 400,000 board feet of oak, mostly from New Jersey, went into her planking. Fir from British Colombia was used in making her spars. The ship sails at better than nine knots and has made 260 miles in a day.

In recent years, this replica has been tied up to a dock in St. Petersburg, Florida welcoming visitors, who may go below to see her 18th Century furnishings, including pewter tableware. They also may see the sailors' hammocks and gear and Captain Bligh's cabin, furnished with antiques.

There is also a replica of the 23-foot boat in which the mutineers set the captain and 18 of his loyal officers and men adrift. They sailed to the Dutch East Indies. The mutineers sailed to Pitcairn Island, where they stripped and burned the ship. There, with some Tahitians, they set up a colony where their descendants still live today. The story of Fletcher Christian and his fellow mutineers is told in the very popular novel, written by Charles Nordhoff and James Norman Hall—"Mutiny on the Bounty," the first book of a trilogy published in the 1930's. The film of the same name, made from the book, was tremendously successful, marking a high point in the career of Charles Laughton, who played the cruel Captain Bligh. The *Bounty* replica made for that film is still in California.

CALIFORNIAN
UNITED STATES

Californian is one of three large, lovely schooners built since 1976 with the guidance of Melbourne Smith, either as builder, in the case of *Pride of Baltimore,* or designer, as with *Spirit of Massachusetts,* or both, as with *Californian.*

She is based on the lines of an 1849 Revenue Marine cutter. *Californian* is a faithful re-creation on the outside. Inside, she meets modern requirements for carrying passengers and also has some touches of elegance, including a governor's cabin panelled in rosewood, and two luxuriously appointed staterooms. The ship boasts furnishings that include antique chairs, sofas and desk.

Californian has a clipper bow with a long jib boom and a figurehead of Queen Calafia, carved by Frank James Morgan. Calafia is a mythical Amazon queen who appears in a 16th century Spanish romance novel as the ruler of an island in the Pacific called California. Like *Pride of Baltimore,* this schooner sets two square sails on her foremast. Also like *Pride,* the lumber for her backbone is a very dense wood from Central America. However, in *Californian,* the frames are laminated, like the roof beams in some modern churches. She wears an iron ballast keel, cast in Pennsylvania. On her transom, she sports an unusual amount of colorful ornamentation, carved in low relief. At the center is a large spread eagle of the type that government revenue cutters displayed. Beside it are the seal of California on the port side and the revenue seal on the starboard. Next to them are two carved bears, facing the eagle. This is probably the most intricately designed transom on any of today's Tall Ships.

As befits a revenue cutter, she carries six bronze cannons. They are six-pounders, used to fire salutes. The ship is used for limited charters, in addition to sail-training, and charter guests are greeted by a roaring salute in addition to the sound of bos'n's pipes, and by the crew dressed in the splendor of period naval uniforms.

The main mission of *Californian* is to provide sail-training to 14 cadets at a time, for 11-day sessions. The vessel sails along the California coast all year 'round, stopping at 15 ports. The concentrated training course covers shipboard safety, standing lookout, marlinspike seamanship, sail and line handling, helmsmanship, meteorology, coastal piloting and use of shipboard equipment. Above and beyond all the proficiency training is the "main course", as on all sail-training ships—self-discipline, responsibility and teamwork. At times, *Californian* makes longer voyages; she has sailed to the Hawaiian Islands. In 1985 *Californian* made a goodwill cruise to Mexico hauling shelter supplies for earthquake victims.

This sail-training ship has a sparred length of 145 feet, a beam of 24 feet three inches and her draft is nine feet five inches. On a rig 98 feet high, she carries 7,400 square feet of sails. She is powered by a 140-horsepower Diesel. The 135-ton ship is owned by the Nautical Heritage Society, Dana Point, Calif.

Gerry Felton

CLEARWATER
UNITED STATES

Clearwater is a replica of the type of sloop that used to be common on the Hudson River about 150 years ago, before the advent of the steamboat, tug-hauled barges, and the railroads. Building the replica was suggested by Pete Seeger, the folksinger and outspoken environmentalist.

An organization of river lovers was created to build the graceful sloop and send her out to carry a message of care and concern for the Hudson's health. *Clearwater* is the flagship of their crusade. Cyrus Hamlin designed the replica and she was built at the Harvey Gamage boatyard in South Bristol, Maine, in 1968.

This gaff-rigged wooden sloop was launched in 1969. She has an overall length of 106 feet, including a bowsprit. Her beam is 25 feet and her mast towers 108 feet. Her owner is Hudson River Sloop Clearwater, Inc., of Poughkeepsie, an environmental organization striving to promote the clean-up of the Hudson, the improvement of its water quality and restoration of the waterfront.

The group conducts three and five-hour educational sails aboard *Clearwater,* with instruction in history, biology and environmental science for children and adults. Their gospel reaches not only the 12,000 annually who get to cruise on *Clearwater*, but the hundreds and thousands who see the sloop sailing up and down the Hudson, or at the many festive celebrations during the year at riverside towns in which *Clearwater* and her crusade star.

DOVE
UNITED STATES

After a three-month crossing from England, described as "boysterous", two ships carrying colonists landed near the mouth of the Potomac River in 1634. They were the 100-foot *Ark* and 56-foot *Dove,* with about 140 settlers who founded the colony of Maryland. They landed at a small bay and called their settlement St. Mary's City. It became the early capital of Maryland.

In 1975, the state decided to build a replica of the *Dove.* William Avery Baker designed the ship and Cambridge shipbuilder James B. Richardson, who had been building wooden boats for 50 years, came out of retirement to re-create *Dove.*

The replica was finished in 1978 and sailed across Chesapeake Bay to her home port of St. Mary's City. During the temperate months, Dove sails around the bay, spreading goodwill and illuminating history with the beguiling spectacle of a 350-year old square-rigged ship. She is a colorful attraction at waterfront celebrations, and a solid illustration that enlivens a visitor's curiosity about the nation's history.

Dove has a sparred length of 76 feet and is 56 feet long on deck. The 42-ton vessel has a beam of 17 feet and a draft of six feet. Her mainmast is 59 feet tall and her sails have an area of approximately 1,965 square feet.

The ship is steered by an outboard rudder, directly connected to a long tiller on the high poop deck. Near the bow, a massive oak windlass is available to raise the 300-pound anchor. The mammoth anchor is in place, looking very impressive, but a modern lightweight anchor is used to avoid the back-breaking toil of handling the authentic but weighty replica. A crew of seven sails the ship. She does not carry passengers.

Dove is a pinnace—a 17th Century three-masted square rigger, smaller than the full-rigged ships of that period, and similar to the galleon, such as *Mayflower.* She is square-rigged on her fore-and mainmasts and carries a lateen sail on her mizzen. The square sail forward is a spritsail attached to a spritsail yard which pivots on the bowsprit. On each of the fore and mainmasts are two square sails. The mizzen carries a lateen sail on a dipping yard—a yard that is always "dipped" or carried around to the lee side of the mast when the ship changes tack.

Vessels with a rig of this type do not sail well upwind, which is why they spend time waiting for favorable winds. They sail well with winds on the beam or further aft. However, in trying to sail up wind, *Dove* cannot come about in less than 120 degrees and makes so much leeway that she cannot make progress, as later square-rigged vessels did and as fore-and-aft rigged vessels do so much more efficiently today.

Dove is colorful to see. Her hull is painted red and yellow at the bow and red and blue at the stern. The hull is heavily built of white oak, and her deck is yellow pine from Maryland. Near the tiller is a wooden binnacle with a candle lantern glowing dimly on a primitive gimballed compass.

Down below, among sparse accommodations for her small crew, *Dove* has a bricked square area on which a fire could be made for cooking. An opening above carries off the smoke.

A considerable amount of research has been done to assure the authenticity of the crew's clothing, and the crew provides an impressive re-enactment of the way sailors looked 350 years ago, head-gear included. The sailors are knowledgeable about their ship and are ready to answer all questions, and to explain the workings and equipment of the ship to visitors.

During the winter months, repair and refurbishment goes on at St. Mary's City.

Jim Wordsworth

ELIZABETH II
UNITED STATES

An account of a 1585 voyage across the Atlantic speaks of "Elizabeth of fiftie tunnes." The ship was among those in three expeditions sponsored by Sir Walter Raleigh between 1584 and 1587, to what is now North Carolina's Roanoke Island, west of the Outer Banks. To celebrate the 400th anniversary of the 1585 voyage, a replica was built. No original plans or specifications were available. *Elizabeth II* is a representative 16th Century merchant vessel, similar in her rigging to *Dove*, the replica of a 1634 pinnace.

Preliminary plans for *Elizabeth II* were drawn by William Avery Baker, who consulted drawings, engravings and descriptions from the period. Final plans and specifications were produced by Stanly Potter. The nine-man building crew, which included two shipwrights who worked on *Dove*, was headed by O. Lie-Nielsen of Rockland, Maine.

Elizabeth II has three masts with square sails on her main and fore masts, and a lateen-rigged sail on the mizzen; she has a spritsail at the bowsprit. Her total sail area is 1,920 square feet.

The "fiftie tunnes" mentioned in the account of the ship's voyage refers to her capacity to carry cargo. Tunnes were 252-gallon barrels.

Pressure-treated yellow pine was used for the ship's frames and juniper for the planking. Juniper was considered more durable than oak in North Carolina's climate. The ship is ballasted with lead instead of the stone or sand used in the 16th Century.

Elizabeth II is brightly painted in blue, red and yellow, in the manner of Elizabethan merchant ships. She is 69 feet in sparred length and 58 feet long on deck. Her mast height is 65 feet, beam is 17 feet and her draft eight feet. Construction was privately financed and the vessel was given to the State of North Carolina in 1984.

Elizabeth II sails with a top speed of about seven knots. She travels to North Carolina ports mainly in the spring and fall, entertaining visitors at her dock at other times at the State Historic Site at Manteo, where men dressed in 16th Century costumes portray the speech and manners of the mariners and colonists on Raleigh's voyages.

FYRDRACA AND GYRFALCON
UNITED STATES

Albert Cizauskas, Jr.

Two replicas of Viking ships are owned and sailed—and rowed—by the Longship Company, Ltd., of Avenue, Maryland, whose members dress in period costumes when they take the ships to historical pageants and waterfront festivals. Designs of both double-enders are based on marine archeological research. Overlapping planks were used in both vessels in the lapstrake or "clinker-built" style.

The larger of the two is *Fyrdraca,* which means fire dragon, a replica of a 9th Century Viking war ship excavated in 1967 on an island in the Baltic Sea. The replica, built in 1979 by Ivan Pederson, Keyport, New Jersey, has a yellow pine keel, stem, sternpost and thwarts, white oak frames and knees, and Philippine mahogany strakes. She has a beautifully carved dragon's head at the high tip of her curved stem.

The 6,000 lb. vessel has an overall length of 32 feet two inches, a beam of nine feet, two inches and draws two feet. *Fyrdraca*'s square sail has an area of 240 square feet, which moves her well downwind and on reaches. She also has 12 oars, each 14 feet long, which are used going into the wind. The crew numbers six to 24 persons.

Bruce Blackistone

The smaller Viking ship is *Gyrfalcon,* a replica of a "faering boat"—meaning a four-oared boat—found with the *Gokstad* ship, a Norwegian vessel believed to have been built between 850 and 900 A.D. based on remains excavated from a burial mound. The replica was built by the Hampton Mariners Museum in Beaufort, North Carolina, under the direction of Geoffrey Scofield.

Her strakes were shaped from marine plywood. The 200-lb boat is 20 feet long, with a beam of five feet and a draft of one foot. Her square sail has an area of 80 square feet and she is rowed by a crew of three to five, with nine-foot oars.

Longship Co., a non-profit educational organization, has trailers for both of these vessels and takes them on cruises, races and other events on the Potomac River and Chesapeake Bay during the warm months. They are docked at Fort Washington Marina on the Potomac, across from Mount Vernon.

Albert Cizauskas.

GODSPEED, SUSAN CONSTANT AND DISCOVERY
UNITED STATES

Three little ships—little for ocean crossings—brought the first colonists to Virginia in 1607, after a voyage of 18 weeks. There were 120 emigrants from England on the ships—*Godspeed, Susan Constant* and *Discovery.* They went ashore at what is now Jamestown and created the first permanent English settlement in America. It started as a fortified trading post. Their thatch-roofed houses have been reproduced at Jamestown Festival park, and replicas of all three vessels are on display there, except when they are out being goodwill ambassadors for Virginia.

Godspeed was commissioned in 1984, after two and a half years of construction. The ship was built mostly of longleaf pine from southeastern Georgia. *Godspeed* and *Discovery* were built at the same time on the same platform. *Godspeed* is 68 feet in overall length, and has a beam of 14 feet eight inches. Her draft is an inch short of seven feet and she displaces 47 tons. The ship carries 17 tons of ballast. Her rig height is 55 feet.

The other two ships are similar 17th Century square-rigged, wooden vessels. *Susan Constant* is the largest of the trio and *Discovery* is the smallest. The 20-ton *Discovery* has an overall length of 49 feet six inches and a beam of 11 feet four inches. She draws five feet and her mainmast is 36 feet two inches high.

Susan Constant is a 100-ton vessel, 110 feet two inches in overall length, with a beam of 24 feet three inches. Her mainmast is 87 feet one inch high and she draws 10 feet six inches. She was built in 1957 and renovated in 1980-81.

GLOBE
UNITED STATES

In 1985, a replica of the brig *Globe* was launched at Sacramento, California, as part of the restoration of Old Sacramento's waterfront. The original brig was built at Westbrook, Maine, in 1833, sailed to Hawaii and later to San Francisco in the Gold Rush era. She ended up with her masts removed and a storage structure with a flat roof built on her decks, and was known as a stores ship. The replica is of that stores ship, not of the sailing vessel. She is a replica above the water line, but below it she has a flat bottom, unlike the original. The new vessel was constructed like a barge. She was built of wood and carries 80 tons of rock as ballast. *Globe* was designed by Melbourne Smith.

The 239-ton vessel is 93 feet six inches long and has a beam just over 24 feet. She will serve mainly as a floating platform which people will cross when boarding river craft at the restored waterfront, which is to have several other hulks that were familiar sights in Old Sacramento's harbor.

Norman J. Brouwe

MAYFLOWER II
UNITED STATES

One of the oldest and most popular replicas in the United States is *Mayflower II*, docked at Plymouth, Mass. She was built in 1957 and was sailed across the Atlantic in a symbolic voyage from England to Plymouth Rock by Alan Villiers, in the path of the Pilgrims of 1620.

The limits on the sailing ability of ships of this type is demonstrated by the fact that the Pilgrims intended to land in Virginia, but strong winds, not errors in navigation, took them hundreds of miles further north. Villiers however, reported that the high sterncastle on the ship did not present a problem in her sailing.

The *Mayflower II* is a three-masted galleon, 65 feet long and 26 feet wide, displacing 180 tons. Her draft is 11 feet. Her rig is similar to that of *Dove*, a pinnace of the same period. There is a small square sail forward on a sprit. Her foremast and mainmast carry two square sails each, and her mizzenmast supports a lateen sail.

Mayflower II's hull has a round bottom and then curves gently inward above the waterline. She has a long, straight keel and a heavy bowsprit, and several ports for guns. The original was launched from Plymouth, England in 1615.

Mayflower II was designed by William Avery Baker, who also designed *Dove* and produced preliminary plans for *Elizabeth II*.

PROVIDENCE
UNITED STATES

The original *Providence* was the first ship under the command of John Paul Jones during the Revolutionary War, and the first ship of the navy started by the American colonies in 1775. She was a sloop with two square sails on her mast and a hull resembling those of square-rigged vessels of the 18th Century. She had a white band along her topsides with gun ports in it.

The replica was built at Newport in 1976 as a bicentennial endeavor of the state of Rhode Island, at the suggestion of Newport historian John Millar. She is 110 feet long and has a mast height of 96 feet. Her mainsail is gaff-rigged, and she has a long bowsprit angled sharply upward, from which two headsails are flown.

An unusual feature of the replica is that she is of fiberglass construction. She sails in Narragansett Bay and along the East coast in the warm months as a sail training vessel and also as a goodwill ambassador for her home port of Newport. Newport? Yes, not Providence.

During the summer of 1984 the big sloop made a 4,600-mile cruise around the Great Lakes for two and a half months, helping to celebrate the 25th anniversary of the St. Lawrence Seaway and the 450th anniversary of Quebec. She also took part in Tall Ships races with trainees aboard. The voyage took her as far west as Detroit.

Norman J. Brouwer

ROSE
UNITED STATES

The original *Rose* was a British frigate, built in 1756 in Yorkshire. Her great claim to fame on this side of the Atlantic was her role in the American Revolution. In 1775 and part of 1776, *Rose* was based at Newport, R.I., as flagship of a squadron sent to prevent smuggling. Colonial Rhode Island's affluent smugglers, who were evading British taxes, responded by convincing farmers not to sell food to the fleet. The British tried to force the farmers to supply them, and the next move was an attempt to fire on the ships with old cannons. The British then closed Narragansett Bay to all shipping. From all that friction came the first proposal to create an American navy in 1775—even before the Declaration of Independence.

Rose convoyed British ships along the American Coast during the Revolutionary War. In 1779, when a French fleet was reported on its way to help the beleaguered colonists, the British scuttled *Rose* across the channel to the harbor of Savannah, barring the entry of the French.

Various pieces of the original *Rose* have been recovered and were used in the replica, built in 1969 in Nova Scotia by John Millar, architectural historian of Newport. The replica sailed out of Newport in the 1970's. By 1980, she was suffering from rot in her planking; in 1985, she was being rebuilt at Bridgeport, Conn.

The term "frigate" in the period of the original *Rose* meant a warship with 20 to 40 guns. She actually carried up to 42. Her replica has a sparred length of 170 feet and a beam of 31 feet. She draws about 13 feet and her three-masted rig, 130 feet high, supports 13,000 square feet of Dacron sails. The vessel displaces 500 tons. The replica was constructed from original plans deposited at the National Maritime Museum, Greenwich, England. Her figurehead is a growling lion—or is it a lioness named Rose?

Norman J. Brouwer

SHENANDOAH
UNITED STATES

Like *Californian, Shenandoah* is a replica of a revenue cutter. She is a topsail schooner setting two square sails on her foremast as well as a topsail on her mainmast. Altogether, her sails add up to 7,000 square feet. The schooner has a sparred length of 108 feet, and her rig is 94 feet high. She has a beam of 23 feet and a draft of 11.

Shenandoah was built by the Harvey Gamage yard, in Maine. She sails out of Vineyard Haven, Mass., during the summer months, taking passengers on cruises and is also used for sail-training for youth groups.

155

SEA LION
UNITED STATES

Seeing a ship replica in his youth gave one man an obsession with the idea of building another—and he did it. Ernest Cowan, like thousands of other tourists, inspected *Mayflower II* at Plymouth, Massachusetts, while on a vacation trip. It struck him that it would be a great accomplishment to build a ship of the same period that would really sail, instead of being permanently attached to her dock. Then, he reasoned, people could be better able to visualize and appreciate what it was like to sail on a small ship as the Pilgrims did.

Cowan did copious research. In 1971, he found information in a treatise published in England in 1586, on the design of the three-masted, square-rigged merchant ship of the Elizabethan period. The *Sea Lion* is named for C.E. Lyon, Cowan's friend, a lumber mill owner who found virgin white oak for the ship's frames and donated use of his mill to cut the lumber. The oak was also contributed to the project. The keel was laid in 1977. Years of volunteer labor and financial contributions from the public went into the realization of Cowan's dream, and huge obstacles were overcome. It has been estimated that 70,000 man-hours of labor were invested in the construction of this hand-made ship.

Sea Lion was launched in 1984. She is about 40 feet long on deck; her bowsprit extends her overall length to 63 feet. The rig height is 58 feet. Her sails, made of flax from Scotland, have a total area of 1,300 square feet. She is a 90-ton vessel, and is one on which a person can indeed visualize how our earliest immigrants sailed to the New World, but she'll never be subjected to ocean waves. *Sea Lion* sails on Lake Chautauqua from her home port at Mayville, New York.

Sea Lion was rigged—another major undertaking—using 9,000 pounds of hemp line from Denmark. She was commissioned in the summer of 1985 and tested under sail. She is owned by Sea Lion Project Limited, a membership organization the public is invited to join. The address is: R.D., One Sea Lion Drive, Mayville, N.Y. 14757. *Sea Lion* swings on a mooring firmly chained to a burial vault that contains four tons of concrete.

Apprenticeshops

The skills required to build wooden ships by traditional methods are being taught to young people in the United States at several locations, notably at two "apprenticeshops" in Maine, at Rockport and Bath. Visitors are welcome at both. The Rockport shop has a gallery from which observers can watch the work going on below. The same shop has the 36-foot Maine pinky schooner *Perseverance*, which was finished there in 1984 and sailed to Newport just in time to be a belle at the Wooden Boat Show. She displays the usual "back porch" of a pinky—a sharp, overhanging stern.

Summer visitors to Rockport Harbor, where the apprentices sharpen their skills, are likely to see other schooners based there as part of the Maine windjammer passenger-carrying fleet. Among these is the 70-foot schooner *Timberwind*.

During 1985-86, the Rockport apprentices were building two pulling boats based on a 18th Century French design. The shop has 14 apprentices at a time and makes an effort to have some of these from overseas.

The Maine Maritime Museum at Bath also operates an apprenticeshop, building traditional vessels and passing on to young people the knowledge and skillful handwork of the old time builders of wooden watercraft.

The double-ended schooner *Vernon Langille*, built by the apprentices in 1978-79 and used for sail training, was sold in 1985. That same year, after three years of construction, the apprenticeshop launched the 53-foot pinky *Maine*, named for one of the last pinky schooners that worked in Maine. The original was built in Essex, Massachusetts, in 1845.

The apprenticeshop at Bath trains 12 apprentices at a time. They pay no tuition, but must perform certain work for the museum. They bring their own tools and drafting equipment, support themselves, and must post a deposit of $1,000, which is returned with interest at the end of the 18-month apprenticeshop program. The deposit may be forfeited if the apprentice cancels or fails to meet his or her obligations.

The training program covers small boat construction, features of large vessel construction, repair and restoration, operation of a boatshop, record keeping and estimating, lofting and drafting, and other subjects related to watercraft.

Apprentices are taught wooden boat building at other locations, including the North Carolina Maritime Museum at Beaufort.

Elements not listed on any apprenticeshop curriculum, but highly evident to anyone who watches apprentices work, are a tremendous pride in work well done, an almost reverential regard for careful boat building, and consideration and respect for each other's skills.

Kip Brundage, Rockport Apprenticeshop

Kip Brundage, Rockport Apprenticeshop

Shipbuilding and Restoration Projects

For some, the excitement of being at a gathering of Tall Ships is enough. For others, visiting a maritime museum satisfies curiosity. For still others, enthusiasm for being a part of something bigger than themselves inspires big dreams and real-life projects alike.

Groups of such dreamers and builders have gathered at workshops and docksides across the country to build Tall Ships and replicas of their own. With excellent scholarship, painstaking detail work and attention to historical accuracy, they are challenged by the task of constructing vessels that match the qualities of the past with the legal requirements of sailing in the present. In most cases, they welcome public visits and support.

The American Clipper

Wilmington, Delaware

Of all the current Tall Ships projects, the grandest in its vision is the clipper concept of Captain Charles M. Quinlan, who lives on his 1934 yawl at Wilmington, Delaware, where he directs the effort to build a replica of Sweden's *Kalmar Nyckel.*

Quinlan's clipper project is a noble idea. It calls for building a clipper ship not as a replica, but as the "next American clipper," following in the tradition of the best clippers of the creative surge of shipbuilding in the last century.

"The clipper ship is the strongest symbol of Americanism," Quinlan believes. The American clippers, he says, were the most magnificent vessels ever to sail. They demonstrated what Americans could accomplish in the arts and sciences of naval architecture, wooden shipbuilding, sailing and navigation. They were masterpieces of incredible beauty, outside and inside. Their majestic grace under sail is well recognized, but less known are their gorgeous interiors, ornamented with zebra wood, butternut, rosewood and other handsomely grained and rare woods. Beyond their beauty, they are symbols of American nation-building and individual enterprise, and heroic reminders of the nation's glorious maritime heritage.

The captain pictures the new clipper as a national monument dedicated to the daring and discipline of the builders, captains and crews who created a merchant marine that was the envy of the world.

With an estimated cost of $25 million to build the vessel and sail her around the world, she will be a magnificent ship of the *Flying Cloud* class, with a sparred length of about 225 feet. She is meant to be a Tall Ship representing the people of the United States and bearing the fitting name: *Shining Sea.*

The last American clipper went down in 1920. The only clipper known to exist now is the British *Cutty Sark*, a museum ship at Greenwich, England.

The next American clipper, Quinlan suggests, should have all the modern electronic equipment the originals did not have. He wants to sail *Shining Sea* around Cape Horn on the route the old clippers used, but with the safety of modern navigation, weather forecasting and communications equipment. The voyage will be a re-enactment of the historic clipper passages under sail alone, although the new clipper will have an auxiliary engine that could be called on in an emergency. The Horn will be tackled in summer, not in winter.

Captain Quinlan, an aviator and sailor with long experience in the yacht charter trade and a Coast Guard license as a sailing ship master, wants to be the skipper of *Shining Sea* not only on the trip around the Horn, but on the ship's first circumnavigation.

That is his grand dream.

To accomplish all that, Captain Quinlan has organized a private, for-profit corporation. Anyone interested in helping convert the dream to reality and owning a piece of the project may contact him through Clipper Ship Shining Sea, Inc., Box 25123, Wilmington, Delaware, 19899, to obtain a booklet-prospectus explaining the project.

Black Pearl
New York

Present at the birth and early development of the sail training movement, *Black Pearl* is an unusually handsome Tall Ship of moderate size, and is held in great affection. The ship was for several years owned by Barclay H. Warburton, an outstanding advocate of sail training who was inspired in England to form the American Sail Training Association, of which he was the first president. Warburton bought *Black Pearl* in 1959.

A brigantine designed by E. I. Schock, she was launched at Wickford, Rhode Island in 1951. Now she is owned by the Ship Trust Wavertree, an organization set up in cooperation with the National Maritime Historical Society. The same trust owns *Wavertree*, the 1885 ship at South Street Seaport in New York City. Also berthed at South Street Seaport, *Black Pearl* is to be restored and returned to sail training.

With 1,900 square feet of sails and an auxiliary engine, *Black Pearl* displaces 41 tons. She has a length overall of 66 feet, a 15 foot beam and six foot draft.

Lady Barbara figurehead with model

Lowell Lytle

Ernestina
New Bedford, Massachusetts

The schooner *Ernestina*, believed to be the oldest surviving Grand Banks fishing schooner, is being restored at New Bedford and outfitted to conform to Coast Guard requirements for a sailing school vessel. She was built in 1894 at the Tarr and James shipyard at Essex, Massachusetts, as the *Effie M. Morrissey*. After 32 years of fishing under sail, she became an Arctic exploration vessel and managed to sail within 600 miles of the North Pole. During World War II, she made trips to the Arctic to haul supplies and do survey work for the U.S. Navy.

After the war, she was taken to the Cape Verde Islands and renamed *Ernestina*, for the daughter of her owner there. She carried people and goods between those islands and America and is thought to be the last sailing ship that brought immigrants to the United States.

In 1982, she sailed to New Bedford to be restored. She has been described as the only "Fredonia" type fishing schooner remaining. The *Fredonia*, a schooner with a clipper bow, was designed by Edward Burgess, a noted New England naval architect, around 1890. The *Spirit of Massachusetts*, also a replica, has similar lines.

Ernestina still has cotton canvas sails and hemp lanyards, and carries salt between her frames as a preservative.

The schooner is 152 feet long, including bowsprit, has a beam of 24 feet, five inches and a draft of 13 feet. She displaces 120 tons and carries 8,323 square feet of sail. He mainmast is 112 feet high.

Carving of figurehead

Lowell Lytle

Construction of Lady Maryland Thomas Gillmer

Lady Maryland
Baltimore, Maryland

Built at the Inner Harbor of Baltimore to become a school ship for sail training, the schooner *Lady Maryland* is 82 feet long with a beam of 22 feet and draft of seven feet. She was built at the same place as *Pride of Baltimore*. With a displacement of 78.5 tons and a sail area of 2,900 square feet, the wooden *Lady Maryland* is gaff-rigged, without topsails, and has a large jib filling the triangle before the foremast created by her long bowsprit. The jib sheets go to a club on the aft portion of the jib's foot.

Lady Maryland is a type replica of the "pungys" which served as work boats on the Chesapeake Bay starting about 1840. The design is closely related to the earlier topsail schooners used for privateering and blockade running. Such vessels later became famous as Baltimore clippers. The clippers were larger and deeper than the pungys, however.

Raking masts, a distinctive characteristic of several Chesapeake Bay designs, give *Lady Maryland* a jaunty look. With a round bottom and flush deck, she has four watertight compartments below—one of several features with which she meets Coast Guard requirements for carrying passengers for hire.

Construction of the schooner was sponsored by both the City of Baltimore and the State of Maryland. She is owned by the Lady Maryland Foundation. Built by Captain Guy Peter Boudreau, *Lady Maryland* was designed by Thomas Gillmer, the naval architect who also designed *Pride of Baltimore*.

Galilee
San Francisco, California

The keel was scheduled to be laid in the Spring of 1986 for a 139-foot wooden brigantine to be built at San Francisco by the Call of the Sea Sail Training Project. The vessel will be a smaller version of *Galilee*, a brigantine designed by Matthew Turner and built in 1891.

The new ship will replace *Stone Witch*, the project's former sail training schooner which was lost on a reef off Mexico in 1985. *Galilee* will be a full time sail training vessel, offering youngsters an educational experience under sail.

HMS Hussar
New York

A salvage expert reported in the fall of 1985 that he found the *HMS Hussar*, a 26-gun British frigate which sank in the East River at New York City in 1780. The three-masted, 619-ton ship struck a rock in the treacherous Hell Gate area. According to historical records, the vessel was carrying 80 American prisoners in chains and a British Army payroll in gold coins said to be worth more than $500 million.

The salvager, who had been searching for two years, reported finding the treasure ship with the aid of sonar equipment in water 80 feet deep. She could well be the most valuable Tall Ship in the world.

The Oseberg Ship
Avenue, Maryland

The *Oseberg* ship, built about 800 A.D. according to the evidence of marine archeologists, was excavated in 1904 in Norway. The dating is based on the nature of the carving on the stem and stern. This ship and two others that have been found are believed to have been used at royal funerals.

The Longship Company, Ltd., of Avenue, Maryland, is planning to build a full-scale working replica of the vessel. The ship is 71 feet six inches long, and has a beam of 17 feet. She was propelled by 30 oars and a squre sail 1,001 square feet in area. Built of oak, the ship has identical sharp ends, curving gracefully to scrolls.

The Longship Company owns two replicas of smaller Viking vessels, *Gyrfalcon* and *Fyrdraca*.

Hull of Lady Barbara

Lowell Lytle

Lady Barbara
St. Petersburg, Florida

Lady Barbara is a type replica of a 17th Century Dutch frigate. Under construction in Florida in 1986, the square-rigged vessel is 64 feet long on deck, has a 16 foot beam, and draws seven feet. Her displacement is 60 tons. The ship is built of wood but fiberglass molds are to be used for constructing additional vessels for public use and chartering.

The owner of *Lady Barbara* is Young American Showcase, which formerly owned a replica of *Santa Maria*, used as a museum ship. That replica was destroyed by fire. The firm plans to build another *Santa Maria* for the 500th anniversary of Columbus's voyage.

Pacific Swift
Victoria, B.C.

Many sailing vessels have been named *Swift*, including a brigantine built in England in 1778. In 1986, however, the Robertson II Sail and Life Training Society of Victoria, British Columbia was hard at work building a near-replica with a different rig, called *Pacific Swift*. This version is primarily a topsail schooner, with two square topsails and a fore course to be set in light weather. With the added square sails, *Pacific Swift* may have the appearance of a brigantine with extra sails.

Pacific Swift's yellow cedar figurehead depicts a woman with hands clasped in an attitude of prayer. The ship has a sparred length of 111 feet, a beam of 20 feet, six inches, and a draft of nine feet, nine inches. Frames and deck beams for *Pacific Swift* were prepared in advance and taken to Expo '86, the world exposition at Vancouver, where the ship was to be built.

The Society has two other vessels, *Robertson II*, a Grand Banks fishing schooner, and the new *Spirit of Chemainus*, a brigantine. Both ships are used for sail training.

Young American Showcase

Santa Maria
St. Petersburg, Florida

A three-quarters replica of *Santa Maria*, the flagship of Christopher Columbus, was built in 1976 for Young American Showcase, Inc., a musical production company in St. Petersburg. She appeared in New York in 1976 and subsequently sailed to many cities as a museum ship with members of her crew in 15th Century dress.

The ship was destroyed by fire, but the owners are planning to build a duplicate to be ready for the 1992 quintcentennial of the original *Santa Maria's* voyage of discovery. The replica was 94 feet long, including the bowsprit, had a 19-foot beam and drew eight feet. She displaced 90 tons. The vessel had frames of Florida pine, planking of Florida cypress and masts of black spruce from Nova Scotia. The ship's mainmast, foremast and bowsprit carried square sails. A lateen-rigged sail was on the mizzenmast. Three of her square sails carried large red Spanish crosses. Her construction plans were drawn by James Rosborough of Halifax, Nova Scotia, following information gathered through research in Spain.

Modern features of the replica included a 225-horsepower Diesel engine and a 20-kilowatt Diesel generator.

Santa Maria was frequently visited by school children who, accompanied by their teachers, were taken on guided tours to see the ship's 15th Century furniture, pottery and tools, all of which were recreated.

Sagamore
Portsmouth, New Hampshire

The 110-foot iron ketch *Diana Chris*, built in Holland in 1907, is being converted to a barkentine and has been renamed *Sagamore*. When restoration is completed, she will engage in sail training, carrying about 30 cadets at a time. The work of restoration and re-rigging is being directed by the Portsmouth Ship Trust at Portsmouth, New Hampshire.

Sea Witch
Annapolis, Maryland

Melbourne Smith, who has in recent years designed or built several schooners constructed by traditional methods, (*Pride of Baltimore*, *Californian*, *Spirit of Massachusetts*) is planning to build a replica of the famous clipper ship *Sea Witch*. He expects the ship to be given to the U.S. Navy for use as a sail training vessel for midshipmen of the Naval Academy and of Naval Reserve Officer Training Corps units.

The newborn square-rigger will be built meticulously of wood, using the methods and tools of old time shipbuilders. She will be about the size of *Danmark*—not so large as *Eagle*. Her approximate dimensions are: length on deck, 190 feet; rig height, 145 feet; displacement, 1,230 tons. With 16,330 square feet of sail, she is expected to be a speedy clipper like the original, which often averaged nearly 15 knots for a whole day's run in the trade winds.

The near-replica is to be built with funds from corporate sponsors, who are expected to send her around the world as a representative of U.S. commerce before handing her over to the Navy with a healthy endowment for maintenance. Unlike the Coast Guard, which has the world-famous *Eagle*, the Navy has no square-rigged sail training vessel now, although it has a sizeable fleet of yachts at the Naval Academy. One can imagine that the competition between the services will express itself in races between *Eagle* and *Sea Witch*, as they both take part in Tall Ships races.

The new *Sea Witch* will use modern rigging materials and her blocks will have modern nylon sheaves and stainless steel pins. She will have sails of Duradon, a synthetic that looks like canvas. Inside, she will have watertight compartments, large pumps and a generator to power her full array of modern electronic equipment. Outside, she will have the beauty and grace of the original. At first, the vessel will have no auxiliary power, but before being turned over to the Navy she will have engines installed.

The first *Sea Witch* was built in 1846. Her hull was black; she had a gilded dragon for her figurehead and her masts had a considerable rake. In her early days, she was said to be the handsomest and the swiftest ship sailing out of New York. She was indeed swift; she made one 24-hour run of 358 miles, which was better than steamships of her period could do. On her first voyage to China, she returned from Canton to New York in 81 days. In 1848, she made the same run in 77 days.

The replica will be built at Annapolis on a 14.5 acre site on Back Creek. The State of Maryland has backed the project with a $2 million appropriation to develop the site into a working maritime museum park to be called The Dockyard. The total project was estimated in 1986 to require a budget of $20 million to cover construction, a round-the-world voyage under sail alone in the manner of the original, and the endowment.

The ship will be built by the International Historical Watercraft Society, Inc., Box 54, Annapolis, Maryland 21404.

Vicar of Bray
San Francisco, California

The last surviving ship to take part in the California gold rush of 1849 is *Vicar of Bray*, whose well-preserved wooden hull is lying aground at Goose Green in the Falkland Islands. The non-profit Bring the *Vicar* Home Committee of San Francisco was raising funds in 1986 to accomplish the goal specified in its name, and a survey of the ship was being made.

The historical importance of the ship as the last survivor of those hundreds of vessels that hauled the eager miners to California lies in the fact that the Gold Rush transformed San Francisco very suddenly from a small settlement into a city. Most of the people who were part of the birth of that city came by ship from the East Coast. *Vicar of Bray*, as it happened, came from England and was one of the many midwives at that birth.

This historic ship was built in 1841 in England as a cargo carrier. She originally had a length on deck of 97 feet but was lengthened to 120 feet. She started life as a brig, but was last a bark before her rig was totally removed. She was blown ashore in the Falklands in 1912, and she is still there—now a part of a pier. In the frigid waters of the South Atlantic, her wooden hull has resisted deterioration. The effort to bring *Vicar* back to San Francisco started in the 1960s, but has gathered force since the formation of the committee in 1984.

Stanley Witkowski, Jr., Dupont Co.

PRIDE OF BALTIMORE
UNITED STATES

LOST AT SEA

May, 1986

The graceful topsail schooner, *Pride of Baltimore,* is a replica of the famous, speedy Baltimore clippers of the early 19th Century, but not a reproduction of any particular clipper. The clippers, like other ships of that period and earlier, were built from models, rather than from drawings, and no models survive. She was designed by Thomas Gillmer, and was commissioned in 1977.

The name may truthfully reflect the city's pride in its ship, but it also has another meaning. *Pride of Baltimore* was the affectionate name of an earlier clipper, the *Chasseur,* captained by Thomas Boyle, one of the most successful privateers active in the War of 1812. The ship's achievements were due not only to her speed but to her maneuverability under the skilled direction of Boyle.

Pride of Baltimore is a 121-ton vessel, with an overall length of 136 feet, a beam of 22 feet eight inches, and a draft of nine feet nine inches. Her mainmast is 92 feet high. She is powered by an 85 horsepower Diesel. She is distinctive among schooners because of her sharply raking masts.

Her futtocks (frame sections) were put together with foot-long locust trunnels (tree nails), left "standing proud", that is, not sawed flush with the frames, in accordance with Chesapeake Bay boatbuilding practice of the last century.

Pride of Baltimore was built of better woods than her 19th Century ancestors, many of which were constructed of unseasoned lumber. Machich and bullettree were used for *Pride's* keel; her frames are mostly of Santa Maria, and her stem, sternpost and keelson were carved from bullettree. All are tropical hardwoods. Longleaf yellow pine, two and one-quarter inches thick, was the planking for the hull and deck. The spars were fashioned from Douglas fir. Rosewood was chosen for the tiller and the belaying pins.

A variety of sails on the *Pride of Baltimore* add up to an area of 7,000 square feet. The mainsail, foresail and staysail are made of heavy cotton duck. The jib and square fore-topsail are woven of flax, while the other sails are fashioned from lighter cotton. *Pride of Baltimore* was not designed to carry passengers as she has only five feet of headroom. The ship has made long voyages in her primary mission as goodwill ambassador of the city whose name she bears.

Sail
Training

Ship-watchers can thank the idea of "sail-training" for the abundance of large Tall Ships afloat today. These beautiful vessels, the last great square-riggers and some of the largest schooners on the sea, exist because the many nations that own them believe fervently in the value of "on deck" training for young people preparing for careers on ships in the merchant marine or the armed forces. Most of the sailing ships we admire so intensely are owned by navy and coast guard forces, including *Eagle*, training ship of the U.S. Coast Guard.

Clearly all the young men and women trained on these ships do not plan careers aboard square-riggers. Many leaders of navies and merchant marine services are convinced that serving at sea, under fair weather and foul, is vital training. A ship's officer must first be a fully competent seaman, they believe, and aboard a sailing vessel can learn to be a better sailor and a better shipmate.

Behind that belief is the realization that a sailing ship must be operated in harmony with the wind and the sea, both often unpredictable and sometimes life-threatening. So, learning good seamanship is necessary for survival, and an important ingredient in this learning is the ability to work in harmony with one's shipmates.

For the young participants, the sail-training process becomes an unparalleled push for maturity through the challenge of sharing life in a constricted space and facing the dangers of the sea, where there is no place to run and no place to hide. Trainees recognize swiftly the absolute need to accept direction and instruction, learning to accept the need for discipline among the crew. They realize that each crew member is dependent on the others—all at risk on the sea together often in a situation where unity is required for strength. Understanding the importance of the individual's contribution to the successful operation of the ship, trainees derive satisfaction and pride in their ability to work well for the good of the group, rising to the demands of the situation created by an environment they cannot escape or control.

The concept of sail-training, long embraced successfully as part of career education by governments, has been adapted widely by private agencies not otherwise connected with the sea. Their aim is to extract similar benefits from shorter term sail-training for young boys and girls, usually from 15 to 19 years old. Many of these have heard of the advantages of shipboard experience. Some are looking for adventure; others are attracted to the sea or simply know they like sailing. Still others are special groups, such as troubled youngsters, who are sent to sea on sail-training ships to learn self-discipline and responsibility in innovative programs.

In other cases, sail-training has been combined with education in subjects related to the sea, such as oceanography. That educational experience is offered at both high school and college levels.

Sail-training has also been rewarding when used with physically handicapped persons. The Jubilee Sailing Trust of England encourages able-bodied and handicapped individuals to work side by side on its training vessel. The able-bodied learn from the disabled that one can cope despite handicaps. They all learn to get things done regardless of the obstacles—an essential ingredient of seamanship. In the U.S., on the north shore of Long Island, volunteers are restoring the bugeye *Little Jennie*, with the idea of sailing her with handicapped persons in the crew.

The privately owned vessels in sail-training for young people include many of the most handsome Tall Ships, other than the big square-riggers. Many are large schooners.

An example is *Rambler*, a three-masted staysail schooner, 106 feet long, operated by the Ocean Research and Education Society of Gloucester, Mass., which has a "sail and study" program for college students. It offers an alternate semester of work in the marine sciences for which students receive college credit. Students spend six weeks at the society's classroom and laboratory facility at Gloucester, and six weeks aboard *Rambler*. The vessel takes up to 20 students, who study such subjects as the ecology of coral reefs and the habitat and behavior of humpback whales.

The 130-foot schooner, *Western Union*, is used by VisionQuest, a private agency, in one of its treatment undertakings for youngsters referred from the criminal justice or mental health systems. The organizations states: "The basic tenets of sail-training

—development of a sense of responsibility, rigorous self-discipline, and respect for authority—are the basic treatment aims for a majority of troubled youth." In life aboard ship, the trainees "learn to prepare for adversity and emergency. They learn to function effectively in the most stressful situations, in the wake of great emotion. The youths who have completed the sailing program display a self-confidence and assurance which is evident in those who have successfully met the challenge of the sea."

Western Union goes on voyages. Some of the sail-training vessels go out for weekends or other short periods, and do not venture far from land; others go on longer cruises.

Among the sail-training vessels on the West Coast is *Adventuress*, a 101-foot wooden schooner operated by Youth Adventure, Inc., of Mercer Island, Washington. She carries groups of 25 to 30 trainees who go on weekend sails in autumn, winter and spring, and on longer trips during the summer. Many of the participants are Sea Explores and Girl Scouts.

A 156-foot schooner has been the home of a sail training program for learning disabled students. The student crew of 28 comes from high schools and junior high schools. They receive instruction in marine studies, while experiencing the discipline and cooperation essential for life at sea.

Tabor Academy of Marion, Mass., operates *Tabor Boy*, a 92-foot schooner, on which boys 14 to 17 years old go on three-week summer cruises for sail-training, and for longer cruises in spring and autumn, when studies in oceanography are added to the training.

Sail-training is offered to young persons in Canada, as well as in the United States. Toronto Brigantines, Inc., of Toronto, Ontario, owns *Pathfinder* and *Playfair*, both brigantines operating during the warm months on the Great Lakes and the St. Lawrence River.

The broad attraction of sailing on Tall Ships can also be used to educate the public about the the environment while on short cruises. The Hudson River sloop *Clearwater* is a crusader in that specialized education.

From these examples, it is plain that there are many aspects of sail-training, with learning how to sail as an elementary first part. All of the programs strive to go far beyond training in sailing, to utilize the emotional impact of the sea on human beings, to mold character and to educate.

Sail Training Races

Many of the gatherings of Tall Ships are arranged to celebrate special events, such as the centennial of the Statue of Liberty in New York Harbor in 1986, but many others occur because of races in which the large sail-training vessels compete. Often, schedules are arranged so that the races end at places where a special event is being celebrated, and a parade of Tall Ships becomes a spectacular feature.

It seems perfectly natural that the large square-riggers of the world would race against each other so that their crews could sharpen their skills and enjoy the competition. Actually, they have been doing so only since 1956. The idea for international sail-training ship races was conceived by a London barrister named Bernard Morgan. He talked to many people about his idea of a brotherhood of the sea, fostered by friendly rivalry among the young sailors on training ships.

His crusading drew some enthusiastic followers, and in 1954, Captain John Illingworth, a famous ocean racing skipper, formed the Sail Training International Race Committee. This was the group that organized the first Tall Ships race from Torbay, England to Lisbon, Portugal, and developed a system of handicapping that resulted in the birth of the Sail Training Association in 1956. Illingworth was its first chairman and Bernard Morgan its secretary. The race they sponsored in 1968 drew 17 entries. Since that time the Association has continued to schedule races and cruises for sail-training ships, square-riggers, schooners and others, and to spread the gospel of sail-training.

In 1972, an American citizen, Barclay Warburton, sailed his brigantine *Black Pearl* to Europe to take part in the Tall Ships races. He was inspired to start an American organization similar in aims to those of the Sail Training Association. In 1973, the American Sail Training Association was formed as an affiliate of the British association. It has offices at Newport, R.I.

ASTA strives to get young people to the sea in deepwater sailing ships. The reasons, ASTA says are:

Sail training is an adventure and an educational and character-building experience for young people. International good will results when the sail training ships from around the world are gathered in a spirit of camaraderie and friendly competition. These activities result in greater awareness of, and appreciation for the values of our shared maritime tradition.

"Sail training is an adventure and an educational and character-building experience for young people. International good will results when the sail training ships from around the world are gathered in a spirit of camaraderie and friendly competition. These activities result in greater awareness of, and appreciation for the values of our shared maritime tradition. ASTA organizes sail-training races in the Atlantic and the Pacific, and promotes sail-training on great square-riggers and scores of other ships where experienced sailors offer a combination of adventure and training to young trainees. Membership in ASTA is open to all interested persons. When the Tall Ships assemble for special events in the U.S., whether planned by ASTA or not, that organization cooperates in arrangements to welcome the trainees and provide activities for them."

The tradition of holding sail-training races every two years continues. The Tall Ships races are usually held in even-numbered years, but local races may be added in odd-numbered years.

Races are often scheduled and routes prepared to bring the Tall Ships to a special festival at a port city. This occurred in 1984, when the ships congregated in Quebec in honor of the 450th anniversary of Jacques Cartier's discovery of the St. Lawrence River. And now, incidentally, there is a Canadian Sail Training Association.

At times the squares-riggers and other Tall Ships assemble at the request of others, particularly the various Operation Sail groups which have functioned temporarily to plan and advertise specific envents. Operation Sail '76 brought the Tall Ships to New York harbor to celebrate the 200th birthday of the United States, and Tall Ships '82 drew them to Philadelphia to commemorate the 300th anniversary of William Penn's arrival aboard the ship *Welcome*.

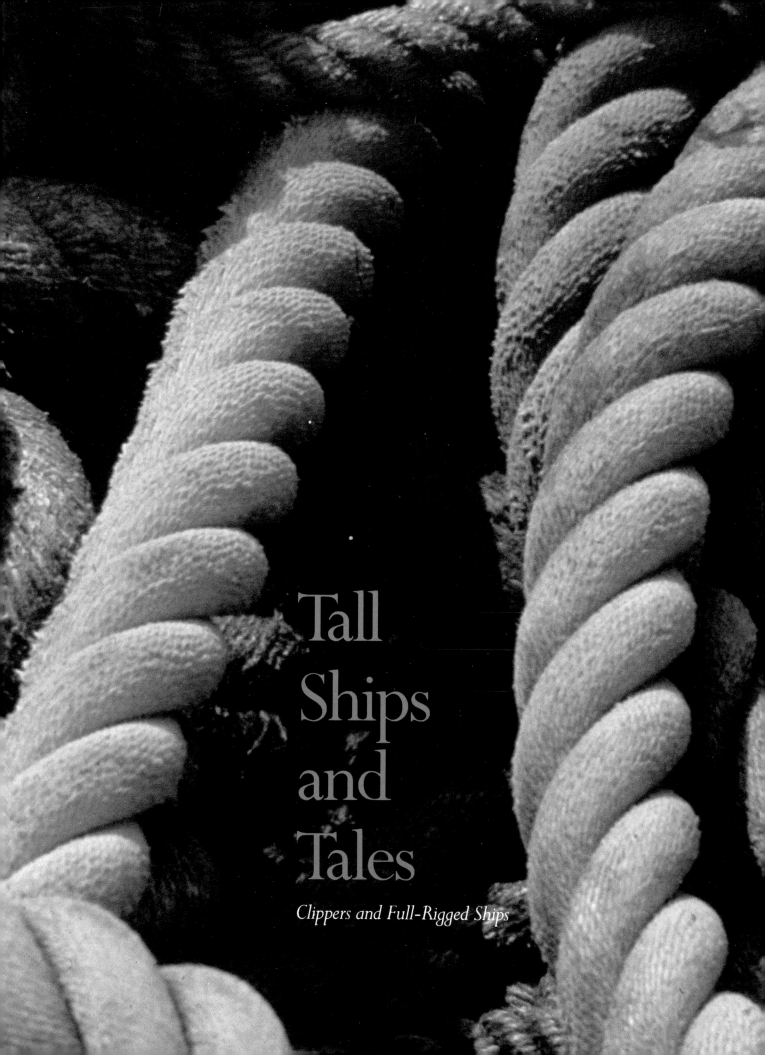

Tall
Ships
and
Tales

Clippers and Full-Rigged Ships

The clippers of the 19th Century that engaged in trade with China often raced home to England and America with their cargoes of tea. Perhaps the most famous of these races took place in 1866 among 16 clippers. They all left a port on the Min River within a day of each other. During their voyage across the Pacific, around Cape Horn and across the Atlantic to London, they lost sight of one another. Amazingly, five of them arrived off the Scilly Isles together and three of those miraculously docked at London on the same tide, within an hour-and-a-half of each other! The three—*Ariel, Taeping* and *Serica*—all broke the record for the China to London run by making it in 99 days.

The speed of those three clippers may be compared with the record of a slower ship, the misnamed *Highflyer,* built in 1861, and also in the tea trade. Her voyages from Shanghai to London required about 130 days.

Another close race was run by *Ethiopian* and *Orontes* in 1886. The two clippers departed from Sydney, Australia together and saw each other several times during their passage. *Ethiopian* won the race by docking only one tide ahead of her rival. On her first voyage, *Ethiopian* sailed from London to Melbourne in 68 days.

Many of the long voyages of the 19th Century full-rigged ships brought disaster or near-disaster in exposure to sudden squalls and gales. *Windsor Castle,* built in 1857, suffered major damage in a gale and snowstorm at Cape Horn in 1871 on her way home to England from Sydney. The mainmast crashed down, bringing with it the mizzen top and badly damaging the bulwarks on one side. Because the mast and its gear were dragging in the water, the crew was unable to steer and waves broke aboard. In great danger, the ship was saved by the heroic work of passengers and crew. The passengers manned the pumps for days while the crew cut the mainmast free and re-rigged the other two masts to permit the *Windsor Castle* to sail. The crew managed to sail to Rio de Janeiro, where the ship was put in dry dock and repaired. 269 days after leaving Sydney, Australia, she finally reached England.

One of the great mysteries associated with full-rigged ships was the tragic end of *Madagascar,* built in 1837. She vanished in 1853 somewhere in the Atlantic Ocean while hauling passengers and a cargo of gold. Some years later a woman who said she had been a nurse on the ship reported in New Zealand that the crew had killed the ship's officers in a mutiny and that the male passengers perished when the crew set fire to *Madagascar.* Young women on the ship were put in boats to be taken ashore with the gold. However, according to the nurse's story, the gold and most of the crew were lost in the surf and only the nurse and two crew members survived. One of those was later hanged for murder in San Francisco and the other could not be found. There is no proof for this story other than the word of the nurse, but there is also no evidence for doubting it.

BANGALORE

Many a Tall Ship has disappeared without a trace; in a few other cases, ships have vanished leaving at least a theory on what happened, even if there is no firm proof. An example is *Bangalore,* a full-rigged iron ship built in England in 1886. In 1908, she left Norfolk, Virginia, on her way to Honolulu with a cargo of coal for the U.S. Navy. She was seen near the Equator, but was never again reliably reported.

A former master of *Bangalore* later said he believed the ship was in a collision off Cape Horn with *Falklandbank,* another sailing vessel which also disappeared. The captain said both ships were sighted near each other in stormy weather, but he did not explain the source of his belief.

The ill-fated *Bangalore* was 260.2 feet long, had a beam of 39.9 feet and displaced 1,743 tons.

The Mariners' Museum at Newport News, Virginia has a quarter-inch model of *Bangalore* by Carroll Ray Sawyer of Manchester, New Hampshire. The museum considers it one of its best models.

BLUENOSE AND THEBAUD

Fishermen from Nova Scotia and New England used big schooners for fishing in those shallow waters of the sea known as the Banks, southeast of Newfoundland and Nova Scotia, and the schooners occasionally took part in organized races. The first one was in 1886 and the last in 1938. The two most famous schooners to vie against each other in these contests were *Bluenose* from the Lunenberg fleet, and *Gertrude L. Thebaud* from the Gloucester fleet.

In 1923, in the North Atlantic Fisherman Races, *Bluenose* was the winner. In 1930, they raced off Boston for the Sir Thomas Lipton Trophy and *Thebaud* won. *Bluenose* won the International Fisherman's cup Race off Halifax in 1931. Their final race was staged in 1938, but unfortunately, *Bluenose* broke a shaft in her steering soon after the start.

So the results were inconclusive. It could be argued that *Gertrude Thebaud* made the better showing, because she was 12 feet shorter and carried less canvas. Or, one could look at the record and argue that *Bluenose* won two to one among the three races completed.

COPENHAGEN

The *Copenhagen,* a five-masted bark, was built in Great Britain for a Danish firm, around 1920 to combine sail-training for future officers of the merchant marine with cargo hauling. This ship could carry 48 students in addition to a weighty cargo. She displaced 4,000 tons.

Copenhagen sailed from Buenos Aires for Melbourne on December 14, 1928, a trip not estimated to take more than 70 days, with 20 crew members and 40 cadets. She never arrived in Melbourne. Although she was equipped with the radio apparatus of her time, she was never heard from. She simply disappeared, presumably in the South Atlantic. Many nations helped conduct a wide search but no trace of the bark was ever found. It is assumed that she foundered with all hands, but what really happened to the *Copenhagen* remains one of the unsolved mysteries of the sea.

DREADNOUGHT

Dreadnought, named after a vessel in Admiral Nelson's fleet and spelled the way that ship's name was spelled, was built in 1853 in Newburyport, Massachusetts. She was a full-rigged ship, 200 feet long, with a capacity of 1,400 tons. She was different from the clippers of her own time in that she was less slender, but she was a speedster in heavy winds and set records.

One is the record for the trans-Atlantic run under sail. She made the run from New York to Liverpool, a distance of 3,018 miles, in 13 days and eight hours. On her first passage home from Liverpool, she beat the Cunard steamer, *Canada,* a paddle wheeler.

But the most astonishing *Dreadnought* record was set in 1862. She sailed backwards for 280 miles! This happened after a monster sea injured the captain; in the confusion no one tended the wheel. The rudder failed and the ship turned her bow to the wind and sailed backwards. The crew managed to rig up a jury rudder and then got the ship sailing again toward a port.

Dreadnought ran out of luck in 1869, when she ran into a calm near the rocky coast of Tierra del Fuego and the combination of the ocean swells and the current put her where every ship dreads to drift—on the rocks.

HMS BEAGLE

HMS *Beagle* was built as a warship, but won world-wide fame in the peaceful pursuit of science.

In her 50-year career, starting with her launching in 1820 near London, *Beagle* made three long, significant voyages for geographical and other scientific exploration. It was the second voyage, from 1831 to 1836, for which the world remembers *Beagle* as the vehicle that carried the young naturalist, Charles Darwin. On that long voyage to the coastlines and islands of the Southern Hemisphere, Darwin collected a multitude of specimens that provided much of the information that he later synthesized into his theory of evolution.

Beagle was a 10-gun brig of 235 tons. No giant, *Beagle* was only 90 feet long on deck, but large enough to carry six boats used for exploration. She was not a rare ship—the forty-first of her class to be built—and by the time she was launched, there was no war to fight. For the first four years of her life, *Beagle* was idle. By 1825, her hull showed signs of rot. When her hull was repaired, a mizzenmast was added to her rig; then she was assigned to work as a surveying vessel. She spent four years, starting in 1826, in the difficult undertaking of charting the waters near the Straits of Magellan and Cape Horn.

During the winter of 1828 the expedition was in desperate condition. Provisions were running out, the crew was afflicted with scurvy, and the ship was suffering effects of Cape Horn's wild winter gales. The distraught captain brought the ship to a small port on the Straits of Magellan—aptly named Port Famine. When the ship was safe he went to his cabin and shot himself.

The replacement was a young captain who re-provisioned the ship and continued the work of establishing precise longitude readings and exploring. He later wrote a two-volume account of the first and second voyages.

Darwin, then 22, was taken along as a naturalist on the second voyage, which started in 1831. In South America he explored the coast, studying plants and animals, and made many journeys inland to the mountains and plains. He found fossils of seashells at high altitudes. On the Galapagos Islands he observed the mammoth tortoises and other animals and plants different from any in existence elsewhere on earth, but related, Darwin believed, to similar species he saw in Ecuador.

When *Beagle* returned to England in 1836, Darwin brought his copious notes and used them to write an account of the five-year voyage. In 1845, a revised version was published as "Voyage of the Beagle." That book brought world fame to both Darwin and *Beagle*.

In 1845, despite her newly spreading fame, *Beagle*'s sailing days came to an end. Most of her rigging was removed, and she was ignominiously reduced to serving as a warehouse. Her ungrateful government owners even changed her name to the bland *Watch Vessel 7*. Darwin published his great work, "Origin of Species," in 1859. *Beagle* was scrapped in 1870 and there are no known remains.

Beagle should have had a figurehead of the dog for which she was named, but there is no record of it.

HERZOGIN CECILIE

Not all the amazing stories about Tall Ships are tales of great speed or mysterious disappearances or shipwrecks. Occasionally, there is a story of a Tall Ship in a violent storm with a happy ending.

In 1928, the steel four-masted bark *Herzogin Cecilie* set sail from the Baltic Sea headed for Australia. She encountered gales off the Orkney Islands and during a furious squall, her 800 tons of solid ballast shifted. The ship was rolled far over to starboard more than twice as far as she would normally heel in a severe storm. Waves were brushing against the topgallant yardarms and the coamings of her hatches were under water. The ship's boats were swept overboard or smashed.

Cecilie was in immediate danger of turning over; apparently it was only her 600 tons of water ballast that prevented the sand ballast from capsizing the ship. Fortunately, she had been running with shortened sails. The few sails that were set quickly blew out, reducing pressure aloft. The ship was lying so far over that the mates ate what meals they could get on the exposed wall of a deck house, and those who had to get from one end of the ship to the other walked on the outer plates on the windward side.

While the main hatches were under water, or in danger of being flooded by waves, there was access to the hold by means of a small lazarette hatch. Captain de Cloux sent his crew below. Everyone,—cook, crew, captain—every able-bodied person aboard climbed down to the hot, dark hold to move the sand, not knowing whether the ship was going to be rolled over further and pushed under the sea at any moment. They literally shovelled for their lives. Planking which had been brought along to repair the poop-deck was used to make temporary terraces to hold the sand as it was shovelled to the high side of the crippled ship.

After hours of grim, desperate work, some progress was made—the ship's dangerous angle of heel was reduced; then, some of the planks snapped under the weight of the sand and the bark leaned back to starboard. The gale worsened; still the crew frantically shovelled, with little food or rest, shifting tons of sand as their only hope of survival.

Little by little, the muscle-weary crew got enough weight over to the port side to put the ship back in a perpendicular position. It required 48 hours of steady, herculean toil to accomplish that. But the ship—and all lives on board—were saved. They had shovelled their way back from the brink of foundering.

FRANCE II AND PREUSSEN

The two largest sailing vessels ever built were both European—*France II* and *Preussen*. *France II*, built in 1911 in the country whose name she bears, displaced 7,800 tons, while Preussen, built in 1902 in Germany, displaced 5,081 tons. The two behemoths of sail were close to each other in sparred length, with *Preussen* at 436 feet edging out *France II* at 420 feet. Their beams were about the same: 53 feet for the French ship and 52 feet for *Preussen.*

They share honors and fates. The French vessel is the record holder as the largest sailing ship ever built, while the German ship holds the record as the largest full-rigged ship ever built. In addition, *Preussen* was the only five-masted full-rigged ship. *France II* was also five-masted, but she was rigged as a bark.

The two were unquestionably big, and both got into trouble early and had short careers. The French giant of the seas lasted only 11 years before she drifted onto a coral reef in the Pacific, near Noumea at a time when there was insufficient wind to steer her. She could have been salvaged, but because of economic conditions, her owners decided to sell her for scrap.

Preussen suffered an unfortunate accident of a different sort, also not her fault. In 1910, when she was only eight years old, she was rammed hard amidships by a British vessel whose captain apparently underestimated the large ship's speed. The accident occurred in the English Channel, and *Preussen* was towed to a harbor, but was never repaired.

Both five-masters deployed vast areas of sail. *France II* flew more than 68,000 square feet—about an acre and a half, and could make 16 to 17 knots with her 32 sails. *Preussen* put up 59,000 square feet in 30 sails, and was credited with 16 knots.

As products of the 20th Century, both ships had steam power aboard, too, and therefore required small crews. Both used steam power on deck to move the heavy sails and yards. *Preussen* had an ingenious arrangement to swing the three lowest yards at the same time when the ship tacked. *France II* had four steam-powered winches to handle cargo at her four hatches. She required a crew of only 45; *Preussen* was manned by 46. Both were designed to compete on long hauls with steamships as freighters and passenger carriers.

Preussen sailed from Hamburg to a port in Chile in 57 days in 1903, setting a record.

France II could take on more than 78,000 cubic feet of water ballast when she had to sail without a cargo. She had about 30 miles of running rigging. Her mainmast was 210 feet above the waterline. *Preussen*'s was even higher–225 feet.

MARY CELESTE

The fate of the brigantine *Mary Celeste* is one of the long-standing mysteries of the sea which will probably never be solved. It all started in 1872. *Mary Celeste* and another brigantine, *Dei Gratia,* from Nova Scotia, left New York 10 days apart, both headed for the Mediterranean. As *Dei Gratia* neared Gibraltar on December 4, her crew was astonished to see *Mary Celeste,* under short canvas, apparently drifting.

The captain of the *Dei Gratia,* noting that not only was she adrift, but no one was visible on deck, sent the first mate and two seamen in a small boat to check on the other ship. They found the ship was abandoned, her lifeboat was missing. Checking further, they found the ship was in seaworthy condition, and her log had no entries after November 24–ten days before the crew from *Dei Gratia* came aboard.

Everything was not shipshape on board *Mary Celeste,* but there were no signs of violence or struggle or any clear indication of what would make her crew abandon the ship. Her cargo, barrels of alcohol, was slightly damaged. The binnacle was out of place and broken. The chronometer and sextant were missing. There was still food and drink among the ship's supplies. There was some sea water in the hold, but not a dangerous amount.

The Nova Scotians of the *Dei Gratia* decided to sail *Mary Celeste* to Gibraltar, where an official inquiry was conducted. An investigator found stains, but analysis determined that they were not blood. The investigation resulted in no answer to the questions that have persisted ever since: Why was the ship abandoned?

What happened to the crew?

THOMAS W. LAWSON

At the beginning of the 20th Century, schooners found profitable work in hauling coal. More than 50 five-masted schooners were built as coal ships, and 10 six-masted schooners were built in the early 1900's. The *Thomas W. Lawson,* launched at Quincy, Mass., in 1902, went them one better; she actually had seven masts. As was usual with schooners with three or more masts, all were the same height and all were gaff-rigged with topsails.

The steel-hulled *Lawson* was a record breaker; she was the only seven-master ever built. She was 395 feet in overall length–extremely long, but not so long as a few ships built later. She could haul 9,000 tons of coal.

After working four years at the job for which she was built, *Lawson* switched fuels, becoming an oil tanker under sail–a rare status. In 1907, only five years after she first sailed, *Lawson* suffered an ignominious accident. While anchored in the Scilly Isles, off England's southwest coast, she was hit by a gale and driven onto a reef, where she sank.

PAMIR

One of the last steel-hulled four-masted ships ever built, *Pamir* was launched in 1907, at a time when steamships were dominating the ocean freight business. She was a bark more than 300 feet long and therefore not in a class with those giant five-masters, *France II* and *Preussen,* which were also built in this century. *Pamir* displaced 4,670 tons—considerably less than the others.

While the other two had short lives due to misfortune, *Pamir* worked for more than 30 years as a cargo vessel. In the early part of her career, she sailed to Chile for nitrates; later, she hauled freight between Europe and Australia.

Pamir was built for the German shipping firm of F. Laeisz, whose vessels all had names starting with the letter P. *Preussen* was one. Another is *Peking,* which survives today and is a prime attraction at South Street Seaport in New York City. Laeisz called his ships the Flying P Line of Hamburg.

In 1950, *Pamir* was abondoned in Antwerp, Belgium. The German government bought her and converted her to new use as a training ship, after installing an auxiliary engine. She was again being used as a cargo vessel and was carrying grain in 1957, when she was struck by a hurricane in the Atlantic Ocean. *Pamir* was blown over and she sank with her crew of 80—joining the hundreds and hundreds of sailing ships that lost their duels with storms at sea.

VASA

One of the worst performances ever made by a ship was turned in by the famous Swedish galleon *Vasa.* She sank on her maiden voyage when the first gust of wind hit her. That was on August 10, 1628.

Sweden was at war and the king had ordered a fine new ship. The Dutch-designed *Vasa* was to be the answer—230 feet long, including bowsprit, and 35 feet wide, a ship displacing 1,400 tons. She was heavily armed with many cannons and mortars and carried 133 seamen and 300 soldiers. Some of those cannons apparently put too much weight too high.

She was expensively built, with many relief carvings and pieces of sculpture in gilded wood. *Vasa* was designed to be very high; her sterncastle rose about 50 feet above the waterline.

She was towed out into the harbor for her maiden voyage. She started raising her sails when a gust of wind struck her starboard side and heeled her over, far enough for water to enter through her open gun ports. Within a few minutes, the great new ship sank in 100 feet of water. *Vasa* was rescued from the water in 1961, 333 years after her failed sea trials.

Today, *Vasa* is amazingly preserved. The combination of cold, fresh water and the kind of mud in which shipworms cannot live saved much of the hull. Also preserved were parts of the bodies, clothing and possessions of the men and women who were aboard, giving valuable insights into Swedish life hundreds of years ago.

A FINAL STORY

Many entertaining yarns have been spun from the days of the sailing ships. Here's our favorite:

The captain served as well as he could as the ship's doctor, using a medicine chest with numbered bottles and a label pasted inside the lid which listed the ailments for which each bottle was to be used.

One day, a seaman came to the old man with an ailment that called for a dose from the #9 bottle. Unfortunately, that bottle was empty. But the resourceful captain made his medical decision. He gave his patient a mixture of #4 and #5.

One hopes it added up to an effective treatment.

Gifts From The Sea

Long before the advertising business and the age of computers came along to modify, enrich or pollute the English language, sailing brought nautical words and phrases ashore. Some, in direct translation, became basic vocabulary for later means of transportation.

Some examples:

All aboard became the train conductor's call announcing a train's departure. Cargo is *shipped* by train.

A train is said to have regular *runs;* for example, the New York to Chicago run.

Caboose, the last car on a freight train, reserved for the crew, is derived from the same word used by the British for a ship's galley; from the Dutch *kamboos,* for galley.

Ballast on railway tracks comes from the same word for material used to steady a ship when cargo was removed from the ship's hold. Original rail ballast may have been the same as ship's—gravel and sand.

A *tender* is a coal car attached to the locomotive. On the sea it is a small boat serving a ship.

We also speak of a *fleet* of buses. *Pilots,* like those who steered the course for ships, fly airplanes. We may *charter* a plane or a bus. A plane's *steward* welcomes passengers *aboard.* The list can be expanded easily. Try it yourself!

More interesting is the figurative translation from sea to shore that adds spice to everyday speech. Here are a few examples:

ASHORE	AT SEA
In the doldrums State of depression or inactivity.	A belt of calms and rainy weather near the equator.
A clean sweep To make a fresh start; get rid of everything.	A sea breaking over the rail, washing overboard all movable objects.
Carrying coals to Newcastle Any superfluous undertaking.	Newcastle is a North Sea port, where the main industry was mining and exporting coal.
Barge into To butt in rudely.	From accidents when canal barges bumped into other boats.
Bear down upon To put pressure on.	To sail toward another vessel from a position upwind.
Figurehead A person holding office whose name or fame is used for display purposes.	A decorative carving on a ship's bow.
Act of God Not covered by insurance; circumstances beyond control.	First used in marine insurance; same meaning.
Graveyard shift Midnight work shift; used in many fields of industry.	*Gravy-eye watch:* From midnight to 4am, when eyes felt sticky from sleep.
To reel off, *Right off the reel* To list or recite something quickly, without stopping, e.g. "He produced the projected figures right off the reel."	From an old device used to measure the speed of a ship; a block was attached to a marked line that was wound on a spinning reel. When a ship was going fast, the reel made a humming sound.

Spin a yarn
Tell a tall tale or story.

Making spun yarn from untwisted rope, two sailors worked together to operate a small winch. They lightened the tedious task with conversation or storytelling—spinning a yarn.

Son of a gun
Slang: rascal; e.g. "You old son of a gun!"

The favored place on a warship for a woman in labor to go for delivery was the space between broadside guns. A child born there was called a son-of-a-gun. If a woman was in labor for a long time, the surgeon might request the captain to fire a broadside to leeward, which would speed up the arrival of the son-of-a-gun.

Slush fund
Money that can be for bribes or graft; funds used to "grease the palm" of an influential person.

Slush was the waste fat from the galley used to grease the mast, for ease in raising sails.

Dungarees
Blue jeans.

A Hindustani word, first used to describe sailors' clothes made of blue jean.

Go by the board
To be completely destroyed.

When masts and spars were broken off and swept overboard—a total loss.

Above board
Open; unconcealed; frank.

Above the waterline of a ship.

Taken aback
Taken by surprise; disconcerted.

Said of a ship; unmanageable because of a sudden shift of wind.

Sleep in
Stay in bed late in the morning.

On shipboard, to sleep through one's watch on deck.

All at sea
Feeling of helplessness or bewilderment.

In early seafaring days when navigational aids were minimal and inaccurate, if a ship got blown out of sight of land, its crew was all at sea.

Armed to the teeth
Heavily armed.

A pictorial description of a pirate: rope in one hand, pistol or cutlass in the other, knife between his teeth.

Scuttlebutt
Rumor; gossip.

An open cask of drinking water on old sailing vessels, equipped with a scuttle, for members of crew. A convenient place to pick up gossip and rumor while standing in line.

Shake a leg
Hurry up! Look lively! Get going!

Derived from "Show a leg"! The call of the boatswain's mate to rouse seamen still asleep in their hammocks at a change of watch. In the British Navy, there were often women aboard. If a female leg appeared she was allowed to sleep in; hairy ones had to "hit the deck" or have their hammock's ropes cut.

Three sheets to the wind
Drunk.

Drunk.

Loaded to the gunwales (gunnels)
Filled to the brim, overflowing (a container). Drunk (a person.

In wooden ships, the sheer strake or upper edge of the bulwark or side of a vessel.

Not enough room to swing a cat
Crowded.

The "cat" referred to the dreaded weapon for punishment, the cat o' nine tails.

Slumgullion
Poor quality meat stew.

The entrails and innards of a whale, originally. Later, any distasteful stew.

Aback A square sail is *aback* when the wind is on the side of the sail that will drive the vessel astern.

Abeam At right angles to the keel.

Aft Toward the stern; same as *abaft*.

Alee Away from the direction of the wind. When the wheel of a vessel sailing close-hauled is turned "*hard alee*" or "*helm's alee*," the ship turns to the other tack.

Aloft Above the deck.

Amidships Toward the center of the vessel.

Anchor A device to grip the bottom and hold a vessel by the attached rope or chain.

Anchor's aweigh The anchor is off the bottom.

Anemometer An instrument to measure wind velocity.

Astern Behind the ship; backwards.

Athwart Across the width of the vessel; at right angle to the fore-and-aft line.

Back The wind *backs* when it changes in a counter-clockwise direction.

Backstay A part of the standing rigging supporting the mast from aft.

Baldheaded schooner One without topmasts.

Ballast Any heavy material, such as stone, iron or lead, placed in the lower part of a sailing vessel, or attached to its keel, to increase stability by lowering the center of gravity.

Bank A relatively shallow area, such as the Grand Banks in the Atlantic Ocean near Newfoundland.

Bark A sailing vessel with three or more masts, square-rigged on all but the aftermost mast, which is fore-and-aft rigged.

Barkentine A vessel of three or more masts, square rigged on the foremast only, fore-and-aft rigged on the others.

Barometer An instrument for measuring atmospheric pressure.

Barrel-bowed Nearly circular at the deckline of the bow.

Beam The greatest width of a vessel. Also, a thwartship timber supporting the deck.

Beam wind One that blows across the ship at right angle to the fore-and-aft line. A ship sailing with a beam wind is on a *beam reach*.

Beating Sailing to windward.

Becket A looped rope, strap or *grommet* used to hold ropes, spars or oars in proper position.

Before the mast The sailors living in the *forecastle* are before the mast.

Before the wind Sailing in the same direction as the wind. Also called running.

Belay To make fast; stop.

Belaying pin A rod of wood or metal used for securing the running rigging.

Below Beneath the deck.

Bend To attach a sail to a spar. Also, a knot fastening one line to another.

Bilge The lowest part of the vessel's interiors, where water collects.

Binnacle A box or stand for the compass, usually with lights.

Block A ship's pulley, consisting of a frame supporting a sheave or roller, over which the lines are run.

Bluff When applied to the shape of a hull, full at the bow.

Boat A vessel of indefinite size, usually a small vessel carried aboard a ship.

Bobstay Chain or wire from the bowsprit to the stem to support the bowsprit and counteract the pulling force of the stays.

Boom The spar to which the foot of a fore-and-aft sail is connected.

Bow The forward part of a vessel; opposite of *stern*.

Bowsprit A spar projecting forward from the bow.

Brace On square-rigged ships, a line leading aft from the end of a yard. Yards are *braced-in* when they are pulled athwartships.

Brig A sailing ship with two masts, square-rigged on both.

Brigantine A two-masted sailing vessel, square rigged on the foremast only.

Brightwork Brass kept polished or wood kept varnished.

Bulkhead Partition inside a vessel.

Bulwarks Built-up sides above the deck of a vessel.

Bumpkin A projecting strut at deck level at the stern.

Buntline Ropes fastened to the foot of a square sail for use in furling.

Buoy An anchored float, including those used as aids to navigation.

Cap A piece of wood or metal at the joint between two sections of mast. Part fits over the head of the lower mast; the upper mast fits through a hole in another part.

Capstan A cylinder with long removable arms used to apply leverage in raising an anchor or sails. On modern yachts, *winches* do similar work.

Carronade A short cannon of the 18th and 19th Centuries.

Carvel-built Smooth-sided. Planking edge to edge rather than overlapped.

Cat boat Sailboat with one mast, at the bow.

Cat Head A heavy timber projecting outboard horizontally near the bow for use in retrieving the anchor, a process called *catting the anchor*.

Caulk To force material such as *oakum* into the seams between planking to prevent leaking.

"Charlie Noble" The nickname for the galley smokepipe.

Chart A map for navigation.

Chine Where the topsides meet the bottom, forming an edge in hulls not rounded.

Clew Lower corners of a square sail. Aft lower corner of a fore-and-aft sail.

Clinker-built Construction method in which planks overlap. *Lapstrake* construction.

Close-hauled Sailing as close into the wind as possible.

Club A short spar at the foot of a fore-and-aft sail.

Coaming Raised edge around hatches, other deck openings and doors to prevent water from entering.

Corvette An armed vessel with guns along one deck only. Also called *sloop of war*.

Course In square-rigged vessels, the largest sail, set on the lower yard. Also, the direction sailed is the *compass course*.

Crance A metal band on the bowsprit with an eye for the bobstay. Also called cranze iron.

Cringle A ring sewn into a sail, for attaching a line.

Cutter A single-masted sailing vessel with two or more sails before the mast. Also, a seaworthy patrol vessel, as a Coast Guard cutter.

Dead-eye A round block of wood with three or four holes, through which lines are passed to tighten the standing rigging. Used before *turnbuckles*.

Deadrise The angle at which the bottom of a vessel rises toward the topsides. A flat-bottomed vessel has no deadrise; a V-bottomed one has.

Eye A ring through which a line is passed.

Fathom Six feet or 1.83 meters. Used in reporting depth of water.

Flare In describing shapes of ships, the outward slope of the sides. Also, a distress signal emitting smoke or light.

Flemish horse A short footrope.

Foot Bottom edge of a sail.

Footrope A rope suspended a few feet below a yard, bowsprit or spanker boom, to stand on while handling sails.

Fore-and-aft Along the vessel's length rather than athwart.

Forecastle On a ship, the forward part of the interior, between foremast and bow. (Pronounced fo'c's'le)

Foremast The mast nearest the bow, in all ships having two or more masts.

Founder To fill with water and sink.

Freeboard Distance between the deck and the waterline.

Frigate A warship of the 18th and early 19th Centuries.

Full-rigged ship Has three masts, all with square sails.

Furl To roll or bunch up a sail and secure it to a yard or boom.

Futtock A piece of wood shaped to be joined with other such pieces to form a frame for a vessel.

Futtock Plate The platform of a top.

Futtock Shrouds Iron rods supporting the futtock plate and topmast rigging.

Gaff A spar on which the head of a four-sided fore-and-aft rigged sail is set. The gaff pivots on the mast, which it meets at an angle.

Galleass A warship used in the Mediterranean from the 15th to the 18th Centuries, lateen-rigged on three masts.

Galleon A sailing vessel of the 15th to 17th Centuries, used in commerce and war.

Galley A seagoing vessel propelled by oars, sometimes aided by sails. Also, the ship's kitchen.

Gammon Iron A collar to secure the bowsprit.

Gangway A passage way on a ship or a ladder up its side.

Garboard strake The planking next to the keel.

Gob Line A support for a martingale.

Gooseneck A device for securing a boom to a mast while allowing the boom to move.

Gunwale The rail of a vessel. (Pronounced "gunnel")

Guy A horizontal or inclined support. A vertical support is a stay.

Halyards Lines or wires used to pull up sails or yards.

Hard alee A skipper's command when coming about. See "alee."

Hawse Pipes Holes through which the anchor chain passes.

Head Upper corner of a three or four-sided sail. Also, a ship's latrine

Headsails All sails forward of the foremast. Includes jibs and staysails.

Heave To throw by hand, as in heaving a line.

Heave to To arrange sails and helm so that a ship will head up out of the trough of waves, without requiring constant attention at the helm. A technique for riding out a storm.

Heel To tilt.

Helm The tiller or wheel controlling the rudder.

Hog Said of a vessel's hull when it droops at its ends.

Hold The main cargo space in a vessel.

Hulk A wrecked or stripped hull, including one used as a warehouse.

Jackstay An iron rod at the top of a yard.

Jack-yards Short spars attached to the top of a mast and the end of a gaff to support a jack-yard topsail, a triangular sail.

Jeer A heavy block and tackle for hoisting heavy yards.

Jib A triangular sail set at or near the bow or on the bowsprit. If there are two such sails, the one further forward is the jib and the other is usually called a *staysail*. When there are more than two, terms such as *inner* and *outer jib* and *flying jib* are used.

Jib Boom A spar mounted on the bowsprit.

Jibe To change the direction of a sailing vessel by turning the stern across the wind direction. In a square-rigger, to *wear*.

Jib-headed topsail A triangular sail set between the gaff and the topmast without jack-yards.

Jiggermast The aft mast on some vessels with two or more masts, a yawl or ketch. It carries the jigger, a small triangular sail on the stern.

Jumper A chain from the forward end of the jib boom to the lower end of the martingale.

Jury Rig A temporary mast and spars set up when others have been damaged.

Keel The vessel's backbone from which frames rise like ribs.

Ketch A two-masted vessel with foremast the taller and mizzen forward of the rudderpost.

Knot A measure of speed. One knot is one nautical mile per hour.

Ladder A ship's stairs.

Lateen A triangular sail on a long yard set at an angle of about 45 degrees to the deck.

Lanyard A rope reeved through the deadeye to tighten the rigging. Or, a line used to make anything fast–even a short line to secure a knife.

Lapstrake A method of boatbuilding in which the planks overlap. See *clinker*.

Latitude Distance north or south of the equator, expressed in degrees.

Lead A piece of lead on a line for measuring the depth of the water. "Heave the lead" means to take a sounding, to measure the depth.

Lee The side of a vessel away from the direction in which the wind is blowing. Also, *leeward*.

Leech The aft edge of a triangular sail, or side of a square sail. Also spelled *leach*.

Lee Shore Shore with the wind blowing toward it; the shore that lies leeward of the vessel.

Letter of marque License granted to a privateer to plunder enemy commerce.

Longitude Distance east or west of the meridian through Greenwich, England.

Loose-footed sail A sail whose foot is not attached to a boom all along its length.

Luff The forward edge of fore-and-aft sail. As a verb, to bring the vessel too close to the wind, so that the sails shake.

Mainmast The highest mast on a vessel or the center mast on a three-masted vessel.

Mainsail Largest sail on mainmast.

Main Royal Fifth level sail, below skysail.

Manrope A safety rope at the side of a ladder or gangway.

Martingale A short spar pointing down beneath the bowsprit. Also called *dolphin striker*.

Martnets Leechlines on a square sail.

Mizzen On a three-masted vessel, the aftermost mast. On a ketch or yawl, the aft mast or sail.

Moon-Raker In old sailing ships, a small sail set above the skysail. Also called *Moon-sail*.

GLOSSARY

Nautical Mile 1852 meters or 6,076.1 feet; about 1.15 statute miles.

Oakum Fiber from old ropes used for caulking.

Off Soundings In water more than 100 fathoms deep.

Orlop Deck The lowest deck.

Overall Length In legal terms, the length of a vessel from tip of the stem to the aftmost part of the stern. In this book, sparred length.

Parcel To wind strips of canvas tightly around wire or rope as part of the process of worming, parceling and serving.

Parrel A sliding collar of rope, metal or wood, holding a yard to the mast allowing vertical movement.

Peak Upper and outer corner of a gaff-rigged fore-and-aft sail.

Pink or Pinky A vessel with a narrow "pinked," overhanging stern.

Pinnace 17th Century three-masted square-rigger.

Point One of 32 points of the compass. 11¼ degrees. As a verb, to sail close to the wind.

Poop A raised deck at the stern of a vessel.

Pooped A vessel is pooped when a following sea breaks over the stern.

Port Left side.

Privateer A vessel commissioned to prey on enemy commerce.

Quarter Aft side, as in port quarter.

Raffee A triangular topsail set from the truck and yardarms of the highest yard.

Rail The top of the bulwarks.

Raise To "raise a light" is to see it.

Rake Angle. A raked mast slopes.

Ratlines Rope rungs seized to the shrouds, forming a ladder for climbing aloft. (Pronounced "ratlins")

Ready about Preparatory command before "Hard alee" or "Helm's alee" in tacking.

Reef To reduce exposed sail area.

Reef points Lines placed in a series parallel to a boom or yard for fastening a reefed sail.

Rig The arrangement of a vessel's masts and sails.

Rigging All the lines and their fittings on a vessel. The standing rigging supports the mast or masts. The running rigging raises, lowers and controls the sails.

Robands Small lines used to tie a square sail to a jackstay.

Royal On a square-rigged vessel, the sail above the topgallant sail.

Schooner A fore-and-aft rigged vessel, with two or more masts, the second carrying the mainsail.

Serving Winding thin line, such as *marline* (called *small stuff*) tightly around a rope or wire. Often done with the aid of a *serving mallet,* a simple device for pulling the line tight.

Sheer The line, usually curved, of a vessel's side from fore to aft.

Sheet A line used to control the position of a sail.

Ship A full-rigged ship or ship-rigged vessel to some. More generally, any vessel.

Shipwright A skilled builder of vessels.

Shrouds Lines or wires from the masthead to the side of the vessel to support the mast as part of the standing rigging.

Skipper Master of a vessel, especially a yacht.

Skysail A light sail above the royal on a square-rigged vessel.

Sloop A single-masted sailing vessel with one headsail.

Sound To measure the depth of water.

Spanker A gaff-rigged fore-and-aft sail at the stern of a bark or a full-rigged ship.

Spar A mast, boom, yard or other support for sails, originally of wood.

Spinnaker A large, lightweight three-cornered sail set on the foremast for sailing downwind.

Spritsail A four-sided sail stretched by a spar called the *sprit,* extending from the peak diagonally to the mast near the deck.

Squaresail A four-sided sail hung from a spar called a yard.

Starboard Right side.

Stay A line or wire supporting a mast from its front (forestay) or back (backstay).

Staysail A sail set on a stay.

Stem The fore part of a vessel's bow joining the keel.

Stern The after part of a vessel.

Sterncastle The high portion of the stern of medieval ships.

Strakes Planks of a vessel's side, running along its length

Strike To lower sail, yard or mast.

Studding Sail Light extra sails, used on square-rigged vessels sailing downwind, set on spars rigged out from the yards.

Tack The lower forward corner of a fore-and-aft sail. Also, to change direction of a sailing vessel by turning the bow across the wind direction. See *jibe,* the opposite maneuver.

Taffrail A rail at the stern.

Tiller A horizontal bar, usually of wood, to control the rudder, for steering.

Top A platform on a mast, supported by trestle trees.

Topgallant Mast In square-rigged vessels, the third section of a mast, above the topmast, which is the second section. The first is the lower mast.

Topsails Second and third level sails.

Transom A flat vertical stern.

Treenails Wooden pins or dowels used to attach planks to timbers in wooden vessels. (Pronounced "trunnels")

Trestle-trees Two short timbers attached to a mast in fore and aft position, to support a top.

Truck A disc at the head of a mast to which halyards are attached.

Try Works Equipment for cooking and rendering blubber on a whaling ship.

Tumble Home The inward curve of the topsides of a hull.

Veer When the wind changes direction clockwise, it veers. Opposite of *back.*

Wear To change direction of a vessel by moving the stern, rather than the bow, across the wind. Opposite of *tack.* Square-riggers *wear;* fore-and-aft vessels executing the same maneuver *jibe.*

Weigh To weigh anchor is to raise it.

Wind Air in motion. Wind direction is expressed as where the wind is blowing from.

Windjammer A sailing vessel, especially a large one, carrying passengers.

Windlass A winch operated by hand (with a crank) or by power, for raising an anchor.

Windward The direction from which the wind is blowing. Opposite of *leeward.*

Worm To wind thin line (small stuff) between the strands of a rope.

Yard A spar from which a square sail is hung.

Yard-arm The end of a yard.

Yawl A two-masted sailing vessel with the mizzen or jigger–mast shorter than the foremast and set aft of the rudderpost.

Yawl Boat A powerful small workboat often carried on davits at the stern of a schooner or other vessel sailing without an auxiliary engine.